when you
pass through
waters

WORDS OF HOPE AND HEALING
FROM YOUR FAVORITE AUTHORS

water books

When You Pass Through Waters/edited by Nicole Seitz
Cover painting, design, and interior design by Nicole Seitz
First Edition, 2015

ISBN 978-0-9969402-0-7

All works within are used by permission of the authors. Grateful acknowledgement
is made to each for his/her generosity. "My Favorite Thing" by Bret Lott previously
appeared in the Jan.5, 2008 edition of the *Charleston Post & Courier*. Batt Humphrey's
excerpt from *Dead Weight* was originally published by Joggling Board Press. Cassandra
King's excerpt from *Moonrise* was originally published by Maiden Lane Press.
Photography: Eva Marie Everson's photo is used courtesy of SON Studios. Marjory
Wentworth's photo was taken by Andrew Allen. Jolina Petersheim's photo is by Heather
Metzler. Fred Bassett's photo was taken by Denise Waldrep. Sarah Loudin Thomas'
photo is by Kristen Delliveneri.

water books

For Eric, Megan, Addison, and Carson,
and everyone affected by the South Carolina Floods of 2015.

PROCEEDS FROM THIS BOOK SUPPORT WATER-DISASTER RELIEF EFFORTS.

When you pass through the waters,
I will be with you...

— ISAIAH 42:3

when you *pass*

Contents

brough waters

*God is here in
the water, in the
trees.*

THE RIVER AND THE TREE OF LIFE

Nicole Seitz

In just about every novel of mine, water is a major thread, a healing balm that pulls the story together. I love to describe the marsh grass and pluff mud we have here in the Lowcountry, or the ocean tides and salty water so full of life. People come from all over the world for the waterways I grew up with and took for granted. God is here in the water, in the trees. It's what I feel when I'm gazing out over sun-dappled lagoons. It's what my readers like to feel when they pick up a Lowcountry novel. With titles like *Trouble the Water* and *Beyond Molasses Creek*, characters like the Water Lillies or Ernest the fish, you'd think I was born in the bathtub. Not quite. Strange but true: *my earliest memory of water was that I was afraid of it*. Water was to be avoided at all costs.

You see, my grandparents' farm in Fort Mill, South Carolina, had a lake in the middle. We had oodles of grandchildren running around, so the adults got together and scared the dickens out of us. They showed us a photo of the Swamp Thing and said it lived in the lake. Needless to say, not one child was lost to that water, though many had nightmares for years to come.

One day, I was eating an orange at the farm when I swallowed a seed. I was only four or five years old, but already I was a worrier. Anxiously, I mentioned the seed-swallowing to my mother. "Well then, you'd better not drink any water," she warned, "or else you'll grow an orange tree in your stomach."

You know where this is going. I can see now she was trying to diffuse my worry by making me laugh. Never in her wildest dreams did she imagine her daughter would have taken her seriously. But I did.

Over the coming days and weeks, I stopped drinking water altogether. I made a valiant effort of it. Soon I began to have stomach aches. Bad stomach aches. I had a huge imagination (and still do), and could *see* that tree in my belly already. Needless to say, I suffered from dehydration all through childhood and by the time I realized I wouldn't grow a tree, the deal was done. I had developed a very bad habit of not drinking enough water, which led me into a constant state of dehydration. Stomach aches. Eczema. Acne. Poor me. My poor *mother*. She had no idea, just kept taking me to the doctor. The funny thing is, my mother is a water fanatic. She drinks it lukewarm so it goes down quicker, and can really chug the stuff like a champ. The other day, I called her at 7:25 in the morning, and she'd already had three glasses! It shows. She's gorgeous with amazing skin, and very healthy. Me? Well, whatever water I do drink, seems to soak in like a sponge. Somewhere along the lines, I must have evolved to have camel-like stores.

To this day, I don't drink enough. When I was pregnant with my children, I got in big trouble with the doctor and was forced to drink these huge jugs of water. I did it for a while. For the kids. But after pregnancy, I went back to coffee and not much else. And then a few years ago, I took up running. Wow. This sort of changed everything.

I decided to train for a marathon. A half marathon first, and then the big one. I'd never run a mile successfully without having stabbing pains in my throat and chest. Let me tell you, running will make your body thirsty, truly thirsty. I guess I'd never been thirsty before. Water was so necessary to the act of running, my body began to regulate itself better. I'd hydrate before and after, but not much during the act of running. I would go miles without it.

And then the big day came. I was running my first half marathon on Hilton Head Island when people started offering me water. The good girl in me, the one that knows how silly it is to avoid drinking water, decided to drink it. Over and over. This led to much pain and torture over finding a porta-potty. You'd think I would have learned my lesson but when I ran the full 26.2-mile marathon on Kiawah Island, I fell into the same trap. People were offering me water. How sweet of them. And food. I started to fear getting dehydrated or hungry. I accepted a lot of it. After several hours and by the last several miles, my stomach seemed to have twisted in two, and I hobbled across the finish line.

What I learned was this. *You've got to run your race just like you train, day after day. Otherwise, you won't be prepared.*

I've seen this truth in some people very close to me recently—my brother-in-law and sister-in-law, Eric and Megan. You see, on the night that the Sawmill Branch Creek in Summerville, SC rose during the Great Flood of 2015, Eric and Megan lost just about everything. Just about…but not quite.

The water came up two feet high and flooded their first floor. The kitchen. The bedrooms. The bathrooms. They'd lived there for 12 years, raised their two daughters there. All of their belongings were destroyed. I was there and saw their faces as they looked at their lives in ruins. I saw a grief I cannot imagine. In shock and disbelief, Megan surveyed her 4-year-old daughter's bed piled high with anything, everything. All ruined.

There was a wooden dresser there. What could we salvage? The bottom drawers held the real treasure, the memories. There were blankets Megan's mother had given her. She wanted desperately to get them out, but the wood was swollen shut. Waterlogged. Armed with crowbar, we pried at the drawer until it opened enough for us to see the blankets were soaking wet. They had been for two days. The water was not fresh, clean water; it was dangerous stuff, filled with bacteria. Fish were found in the living room. Could any of it be saved? I watched Megan's face as she surveyed the damage. It's not something I like to remember.

This was Eric and Megan's race. No amount of training could have prepared them to watch everything they owned wash away.

Except...

They still had each other. The children. They had friends dropping by daily to help rip out the carpet, walls, cabinets. They had loving parents to stay with nearby. They had church friends, running friends, neighbors, and teacher friends, old friends, strangers—*so* many people came together for them.

Right now, it is still too fresh to talk about. They are still in trauma. They've been displaced. All of their physical memories of their life together are gone. But rebuilding will happen soon. Wholeness will come one day. I believe this because I know how Eric and Megan train. They've trained for this every day of their lives together. By being a good neighbor. By being good friends. By loving family. By teaching others. By building up their faith. By growing a network of love and support around them.

Eric and Megan are overwhelmed by the flood, but even more overwhelmed by the outpouring of love they've experienced. Not since the Emmanuel AME Church shooting last summer have I ever witnessed a community come together in such force to support one of their own. And Eric and Megan are only one story in thousands of lives that were interrupted by the SC floods. But there's something special about this state we live in. We train, day to day, with smiles and *how are you's*, investing in one another, so that when the big race comes, we're prepared to see it through, to get to that finish.

One of the best things my parents ever did was choose to raise us children in the Lowcountry. The tree of life is planted by the river bed. My soul is hydrated by the waterways—the rivers and creeks, the lakes and lagoons, the ocean. My husband and I were baptized together in the Atlantic off the Isle of Palms. South Carolinians live by the water, eat from the water. We're cautious of it, respectful of it. And when it storms and water overflows, we get out of the way or pray and bear down. We build our faith by it, faith in one another and in God. He's the one in charge of our tides. And we are the blessed ones to call this place home.

On Wednesday, a few days before the floods, I was sitting on my back porch with my notebook, praying. A book title came to me. I pushed it away. Like a mosquito, it wouldn't leave me alone until I wrote it down.

As the Water Rises

I was scheduled to go on a women's hike on Friday. By Thursday night, the weather men were claiming hurricane Joaquin was off the coast and would be causing rain all weekend. Our hike was cancelled. School was cancelled. By the following Wednesday, I'd seen the devastation up close. The floods hit home with family. And Columbia was getting hit harder than we had. I looked at the words I'd written a week before and knew I needed to do something. I put out a call to author friends to donate their words to help with water disaster relief, and they came through in record time. I changed the title to *When You Pass Through Waters,* a title I felt held hope.

Each author in this book has graciously donated their water-themed stories, poems, and time. Like a winding river their words meander through memories and nostalgia or swell in a fit of faith or questioning. Some offer lessons learned by the water or new beginnings because of it. There are even works of fiction—it often speaks the clearest truth. It is my hope that you, the reader, will enjoy the poems, stories and essays like I have and be filled by them. Be sure to take a deeper look into each author and discover the other amazing works they offer. Our writing community is a mighty deep well of wisdom.

Nicole Seitz is the author of six critically acclaimed novels – *Beyond Molasses Creek*, *The Inheritance of Beauty*, *Saving Cicadas*, *A Hundred Years of Happiness*, *Trouble the Water*, and *The Spirit of Sweetgrass*. Her paintings are featured on several of her books. She is a graduate of UNC-Chapel Hill's School of Journalism, and also has a degree in Illustration from Savannah College of Art & Design. Nicole is a regular contributor to the Southern authors' blog, *Southern Belle View* and has had short stories, essays and articles published in *The Charleston City Paper*, *Literary Dogs & Their South Carolina Writers*, *Lowcountry Dog Magazine*, and *SouthCarolina Magazine*. Her original monologue, "The Longing" was part of *Listen to Your Mother-Charleston* in 2014. Nicole lives in the Charleston, SC area with her husband and two children, and teaches visual arts to elementary and high school students at a local private school. In the summers she teaches youth camps and workshops on global art and creative writing, including a Young Authors and Illustrators camp in which children, ages 6-12, write and illustrate a picture book in a week.

Don't assume that what was ordinary yesterday will be ordinary again.

LESSONS FROM A RIVER

Lisa Wingate

Around here, the weekend started out with a good, slow rain, which we desperately needed. For me, that water song is sweet music anytime. I am a lover of water and have always been. I grew up along a little creek, waking, and sleeping, and playing, and dreaming to its changing rhythms.

After a rain, the man-children and I can never resist checking to see if "their" little creek in the back pasture has risen to temporary river status. These days, we just stand on the bank and look, but there was a time not so long ago when those water levels were critical, all-important, all-consuming. No water meant no swimming hole, no campouts, no fishing, no long afternoons of campfires and hotdogs and s'mores until dark.

Even now, when I visit this place alone on my evening walks and stand and listen as the water passes by, I hear voices. I hear high-pitched laughter and double-dog dares. I hear the splash of inner tubes. I hear, "Mama, I got a fish!" I hear the rapid breaths of a child running back to camp with a treasure found among the river gravel

— a fossil, an arrowhead, a lizard captured in two hands. The very first lightning bug of evening. Do we have something we can keep him in? Or should we just set him free?

This place is alive with memories, but even more than that, it's alive with something deeper. Something longer-lasting. A river teaches lessons. Those lessons become the bones, and blood, and marrow of children raised near water, and earth, and sky. I hope they've been passed to the next generation, these lessons from a river.

Take time to sit and listen. Stop. Stop rushing. Close your eyes for a moment. Listen. What lies beyond the constant white noise? They are there, the transient sounds of life. A bird flitting by, a breeze stirring leaves, a doe passing in the shadows of the wood. The sounds change moment to moment, never the same twice. Everything is passing. The water, the creatures, the day. Each moment is unique along a river. Each moment is unique in life. A moment unappreciated is a moment lost.

Don't be afraid to jump in with both feet. Go for it. Don't let fear keep you on the bank. Trust the water. Trust yourself. To experience something new, to soar, to fly, you must first let go of where you are now.

Look beneath the surface. Don't be fooled by what's on the outside. Look beyond the ripples and mirrored reflections. So much hides beneath the surface of a river. The skittering of tiny creatures, the silver flash of minnows, an ancient license plate washed from somewhere far away, a shimmering quartz crystal, a bit of fool's gold. The truest form of all things is found beyond what can be seen at first glance.

See with new eyes. The river is always changing. It changes with the seasons, with the days, with the hours, with the cycles of drought and flood, with blooming and dying, and blooming again. Where there was bland gravel yesterday, today there may be gifts — a fossil washed ashore, a wild rose bursting forth, a butterfly. Don't assume that what was ordinary yesterday will be ordinary again. Give each day and each season rapt attention. Expect something extraordinary.

Take a friend along. Value your solitude on occasion, but when possible, share your time with old friends and open yourself to new ones. Reveal your secret hiding places, invite others in, offer shelter, offer beauty, offer comfort and companionship. An experience shared is an experience multiplied, a memory made. It is in connecting with others that we broaden ourselves beyond one life into many.

Value the journey. Don't rush. Don't focus far ahead. Look down. Look at where you are. Don't be afraid to walk aimlessly, to feel the water, to let the current slow your steps. The goal isn't to reach the end of the river as quickly as possible, but know the river for what it is, to take in all that it has to offer. Understanding a river takes time. Devote the time that's needed.

Don't be limited by what you can see. Dream, imagine, pretend. Take a creek and create a river. Take a twig and create a boat. Take a log and create a raft. Sail not from bank to bank, but from far sea to farther sea. Take a dragonfly and fashion a dragon. Climb aboard and soar. It is never too early or too late in the day to daydream.

These are the lessons I carry with me as a sudden rain shower dabs the river's surface, chasing us up the banks yet another time. We hurry home, laughing, these man-boys and I. We leave the river and know in some innate way that we'll never see it again. We will come back to this place, but when we do, a new river will be waiting. Water coming, water going, leaves drifting, something growing, something fading.

It is impossible to step twice in the same river. The river is always changing. It cannot be preserved, other than in memory. But the lessons are ours to keep. And in the end, it's the lessons that matter most.

Lisa Wingate skillfully weaves lyrical writing and unforgettable settings with elements of traditional Southern storytelling, history, and mystery to create novels that Publisher's Weekly calls "Masterful" and Library Journal refers to as "A good option for fans of Nicholas Sparks and Mary Alice Monroe." She was selected among Booklist's Top 10 for two consecutive years.

Lisa is a journalist, an inspirational speaker, and the author of twenty-five novels. She is a seven-time ACFW Carol Award nominee, a multiple Christy Award nominee, a two-time Carol Award winner, and a 2015 RT Booklovers Magazine Reviewer's Choice Award Winner for mystery/suspense. Recently, the group Americans for More Civility, a kindness watchdog organization, selected Lisa along with Bill Ford, Camille Cosby, and six others as recipients of the National Civies Award, which celebrates public figures who work to promote greater kindness and civility in American life. Booklist summed up her work by saying, "Lisa Wingate is, quite simply, a master storyteller." More information about her novels can be found at www.lisawingate.com.

*The rain
comes hot with
fury.*

Mama Pine

Signe Pike

This morning moves
like molasses running uphill in winter,
like my father would say,
with everything outside dappled in light,
turquoise stone sky and emerald green
cast against the mottled red bark
of the Longleaf Pine.

She's eighty-years old,
or so I believe,
the seed that sprouted in suburbia,
the cone that grew the pine on this one quarter acre now,
with neighbors and neighbors on
what was once the sprawling farm,
that was once
a plantation,
that once
saw a war,
and before that,
belonged to a gentler sort of people.

Sometimes I wonder
if that isn't why I'm here,

to be gentle again,
to wake this land,
to remember?
I pluck petals from the roses to strew at her feet.
I collect her thorny children and dutifully stack their carcasses in
bags.
In the morning, I greet her:
> *hello, Mama Pine.*
Because trees weather it better than any of us.
Isn't that what they say?
That time never weathers anything well?

II.
Later, there is rain.
The sky goes dark
and the Carolina Jessamine almost burns in the dim
like sweet country butter in the gray swirling light.
The rain comes
hot with fury.
Water rips through the eves in torrents,
the cat curls up,
the dog roots on the couch, looking for her pillow.

When it stops there is nothing but stillness.
The droplets of water
giving way to the quiet,
and the world outside is coated in leafshine.
The pittosporum and the camellia bow,
thick and heavy with the wet of it
that hangs in our Carolina air
soft and worn and gracious,
like your mama's favorite dress.

Signe Pike is the author of *Faery Tale*. The memoir earned a "Best of 2010" nod from *Kirkus Reviews* as well as glowing reviews from *Harper's Bazaar*, *Women's Adventure Magazine*, and renowned spiritual leader Marianne Williamson. Pike has been featured on National Public Radio's "To the Best of Our Knowledge" along with Salman Rushdie, Neil Gaiman, and A.S. Byatt. Her poetry collection *Native Water* published in Spring 2012. Pike worked as a book editor at both Random House and Penguin before relocating to Charleston to write full-time. She is currently at work on a historical novel.

I have found it to be true that disasters bring out the best in people.

TERRA FIRMA

Karen White

I am afraid of water. Some might find that amusing consider-
ing that I make a living writing about characters who live by
the sea, who sail and swim and kayak in waters so deep they
can't see the bottom. Maybe my writing is a way of facing my fear,
although I still can't go into water where I can't touch the bottom.

As a child, I remembered feeling sorry for the itsy-bitsy spider
who tried to climb up the water spout and then is washed away by
the rain. To this day I dislike rain immensely, although this might
be more due to the fact that I lived in England for seven years and
then Pittsburgh, Pennsylvania for three years. I thought that I'd
seen enough rain to last a lifetime.

I also remember childhood visits to my paternal grandmother
in the Florida panhandle with its white crystal sand beaches and
beautiful blue-green water. Sitting on the powdered-sugar beach
next to my grandmother as she told me stories of her own child-
hood while smelling the salt air and listening to the crash of the
surf is one of my happiest memories. Going into the water was
not. This probably had a lot to do with the frequency in which
my older brothers pushed me far offshore on an inflatable raft and
then left me stranded while they pointed behind me and yelled,
"Shark!"

Throughout my impressionable growing-up years my father,
the real storyteller in our family, enjoyed sharing a few harrowing

stories of his childhood during the Great Depression and early childhood on the Mississippi Gulf Coast. He remembered being there during the great hurricane of 1947, before they started naming hurricanes. It was another category five storm, and like during Katrina, the levees in New Orleans were breeched. The storm surge along the Gulf Coast was even more damaging then the 145-mile per hour sustained winds. My grandfather, an employee at the Keesler Air Force base in Biloxi, hid my father, uncle, and grandmother inside a boiler room where they spent most of the night listening to the wind howl and the rain slash at the building while wondering how long it would be until the water found them. It's an image I never forgot.

I was raised Catholic where water represents rebirth and renewal. We are Baptized with holy water sprinkled on our foreheads, and we bless ourselves with water when we enter the sanctuary. It's reverential and pure. It's cleansing of both mind and soul. Springtime, full of birth and renewal, is symbolized by rain. It feeds the fields and flowers, fills the creeks and streams. Yet I could never reconcile this gentle water with the fathomless ocean that could hide large fish with sharp teeth and steal chunks of land in a single storm.

I lived a landlocked childhood, my glimpses of the ocean rare occasions that I dreaded as much as I anticipated. Maybe that's what fueled my perception to almost mythical proportions. If familiarity breeds contempt, maybe the unknown fuels the imagination. My memories of sitting on the shore with my grandmother, the salty-breeze on my face, the calming rhythm of the waves in my ears, battled with the terror of being set adrift in deep water.

It was irrational, I knew. My friends loved going to the beach. And then, as I grew older, my friends continued the tradition with their children. Not wanting my own children to be left out, I began selecting a coastal destination for each vacation: St. Simons, Jekyll Island, Hilton Head, Kiawah, Folly Beach, Isle of Palms. To my great surprise, I fell in love with the Lowcountry. It had me at the first smell of the pluff mud. I'd let my husband swim with the children in the ocean while I kept my feet in the shallow surf. But the marshes were my own discovery. It was water as I'd never seen or smelled it. It felt like home.

I began writing about the Lowcountry because I had to. Whenever a story inspired me, its natural setting seemed to be the South Carolina Lowcountry. I found everything about it compelling: the scents, the natural landscape with its patina of vivid colors, the history, the people. The water. There is something about a place where the land is so close to the water that parts of it disappear on a regular basis with the vagaries of the tides—and about the resilience of the people who choose to live there, battling the water that wants to reclaim it.

This is the land and the people who survived Hurricane Hugo in 1989. With the cost of damage estimated in the billions, thirteen dead in South Carolina, and a flattened coastline, many were left wondering how one rebuilds after such devastation. And why.

When the rains started last month, nobody suspected it would become the "thousand year flood." Residents are familiar with the occasional flooded streets, and most own at least one pair of rain boots, my daughter included. She lives in a carriage house in downtown Charleston, so we weren't that concerned with the news reports of record rain. Even during the worst of it, she could strap on her boots and make it to the Harris Teeter for provisions.

But then we started seeing the news footage of the people bearing the brunt of the flooding, and stories of people losing everything. Of people dying. And our hearts broke. This wasn't a hurricane, so how could this be happening?

I have found it to be true that disasters bring out the best in people. This is especially true in the Lowcountry. Strangers helping strangers, giving shelter and food. Coming together to survive. It seems as if this generosity of spirit and heart is bred into them through the waters that bleed from the ocean and into the marshes and permeate the land. It will be a hard recovery, and it will test their will. But I have no doubt that these people will emerge from this even stronger and more resilient than before.

Three years ago, I bought a beach house. I love the gentle sound of the ocean lapping at the sand, and the feel of the wind in my hair. I still don't love deep water, but I've been known to go snorkeling and kayaking on occasion. My favorite place will always be on terra firma, staring out at the ocean as it cuts into the horizon, accepting that it will always be unknown and mysterious to me—and I'm okay with that. But from my perch I know the magic of the briny scent of the air, the feeling of soft sand between my toes, the gentle swell of waves that deliver a clean slate to the shore again and again. I am home.

I sometimes think that the survivors of storms have helped me face my fear. They are the ones who have taught us how flood waters recede, and leaves grow again on empty trees. They understand better than most why we rebuild. That surviving means much more than simply making it through a disaster, but learning what makes us strong.

Karen White is a *New York Times* and *USA Today* bestselling author and currently writes what she refers to as 'grit lit'—Southern women's fiction—and has also expanded her horizons into writing a mystery series set in Charleston, South Carolina. Her nineteenth novel, *The Sound of Glass*, was published in May 2015 by New American Library, a division of PenguinRandomHouse

Publishing Group.

Karen hails from a long line of Southerners but spent most of her growing up years in London, England and is a graduate of the American School in London and Tulane University. When not writing, she spends her time reading, scrapbooking, playing piano, and avoiding cooking. She currently lives near Atlanta, Georgia with her husband and two children, and two spoiled Havanese dogs.

*Our house is
a river where
books have
gathered in
great piles
along the banks*

RIVER SONG

Marjory Wentworth

Our house is a river
flowing by gardens of fruit
and lavender butterfly
bushes, magnolia and fig
trees tangled in vines that swirl
beneath moonlight and star shine.

Mountain born, granite fed
river of feathers and glass,
where light gathers each morning
and evening as birdsong braids
the air into one green song
humming like a heartbeat.

Passed astonished snow swept
islands and the city
rising at the edge of the sea,
the river rushes in a fury
under the great steel buildings
glowing like ripe volcanoes

in the blue black night. City
of music and light, criss-crossed

with train tracks and avenues
bearing multitudes. City of smoke.
City of dreams collecting
like seeds and scattered on water.

Our house is a river
where books have gathered
in great piles along the banks
before the flood and after,
dog leafed, molded and torn,
tear stained and treasured.

We crossed a bridge and returned
wounded and singing, carrying
butterflies and lightning
in our pockets, children
strapped to our backs, water
rushing beneath us
like an unwritten story.

Marjory Wentworth's poems have been nominated for The Pushcart Prize five times. Her books of poetry include *Noticing Eden, Despite Gravity, The Endless Repetition of an Ordinary Miracle,* and *New and Selected Poems.* She is the co-writer with Juan Mendez of *Taking a Stand, The Evolution of Human Rights,* co-editor with Kwame Dawes of *Seeking, Poetry and Prose inspired by the Art of Jonathan Green,* and the author of the prizewinning children's story *Shackles.* Forthcoming books include, *Finding Grace, The Tragedy and Triumph of Charleston's Emanuel A.M.E. Church,* with Herb Frazier and Bernard Powers, Ph.D. (2016) and *Out of Wonder* with

Kwame Alexander and Chris Colderly (2017). Marjory is on the faculty at The Art Institute of Charleston. She is the co-founder and former president of the Lowcountry Initiative for the Literary Arts. She serves on the Editorial Board of the University of South Carolina's Palmetto Poetry Series, and she is the poetry editor for *Charleston Currents*. Her work is included in the South Carolina Poetry Archives at Furman University, and she is the Poet Laureate of South Carolina.

She holds me up, yet I give her something to lean on.

WADING THROUGH
TROUBLED WATERS

Jolina Petersheim

The picture is taken during our trip out West, the day we think we're going to drown. I am fifteen, and my best friend, Misty, eighteen. The photo's backdrop is my family's ancient, dust-crusted, black conversion van. Our arms are folded with my shoulder tucked beneath hers. Our faces are frozen in the moment between attempted sultriness and uncontainable mirth. Misty's face is shadowed by the brim of her Cody, Wyoming cowboy hat she bought at the rodeo the night before. The pucker of her pout is the only thing truly perceived. I am wedged into Wranglers I have owned before I knew puberty was even a word–apparently, I do not care to breathe.

Our cowgirl gear makes us adventurous; our bravado like a rodeo clown's dodging the horns of a thrashing bull. For the past five days, our eyes have been drawn to the crater-like mountains that arch over us with as much mystery as the dark side of the moon. The only thing that lies in the way of our Lewis and Clark exploration is a seething river that slices through the untamed terrain. With my parents and younger brother in town, we are deafened to all rationality by our clanging excitement. We pick our way down to the river and realize we've got company. A lone cowboy from a distant ranch with a name I cannot remember and a camel-like face I cannot forget, reassures us in a low twang, "If anything goes wrong with you girls, I'll fish ya out for sure."

With this, we are encouraged to begin. Clasping hands, we solemnly nod before wading into the depths of the Grey Bull River. After only three steps, the water sloshes against our thighs, wobbling our weight as our feet strive to find placement on the smooth stones. Misty moves in front, each step taken on slow shutter speed. My fear heightens as the water rises and pounds against my thundering heart. Each step I take, I am sure will be the one that sweeps me downstream as if I am nothing more than a leaf.

Without turning, I yell to the cowboy, "You can swim, right?"

His long pause causes me to angle my head to watch him out of my peripheral vision. He takes off his battered hat and scratches his scalp with dirty nails. "Well, I can't say I can swim, but I can come getch ya if ya need it."

Misty and I stand stock still. The water growls as it surges around us. Misty glances behind her and our eyes lock. Fear glows there as if she is watching her life flutter by, carried by a current.

"Let's go back."

Her words are whipped into whispers, but I understand.

Slowly, ever-so-slowly, I turn around. My new Timberlands slide and shiver over the rocks. My mind and body feel numb. The cowboy squats stupidly on the bolder-speckled shore, picking his teeth with a piece of straw. I glance behind me to watch Misty's progress. She moves with as much trepidation as I do. I begin begging the Lord to let us live to a ripe old age. I pray that He'll let us sit on white-washed rockers on our front porch, sipping tea while we fondly reminisce about these adventures instead of joining Him early because of them.

Unable to find my footing, I falter and clatter over the stones. Suddenly, Misty is there, her palm against my spine, buoying me up, giving me the strength to continue. She holds me up, yet I give her something to lean on. Together, we make it across the treacherous torrent and collapse onto the shore.

Spring 2006

Misty swerves across four lanes of Nashville traffic, her green Honda lurching over the hump in the concrete. She moves forward to park but shifts into reverse after reading the "For Patients Only" sign.

"I don't want to park here…at least for today," she quips.

I try to smile, but find it difficult. My hands are shaking as I unfasten my seatbelt and grab my purse. A shuttle for chemotherapy patients careens to a stop in front of the American Cancer Society entrance.

The driver is smoking.

Inside, a glass partition separates one department from another, hiding nothing of what is transpiring within. Rows of patients with shadow-rimmed eyes and gaunt cheeks sip carbonated beverages while poison seeps into their bloodstream. They flip through magazines and watch daytime soaps until the cresting waves of nausea overwhelm them with as much force as a tsunami.

It is then that I must turn away.

I stand close to Misty to feel her radiating warmth, to know she is still there. She asks the nurse, "May we look at the wigs, please?"

Like a hostess leading us to our table, the nurse smiles and chatters while maneuvering us through the corridor. The colors are mauve and cream, the lighting low. There are no pictures on the walls. Maybe the patients would become bitter if their time here appeared normal when it so obviously is not.

The nurse makes a sudden shift to the left, wedging her key into the lock. She twists the knob and thrusts it open with an ample hip. For but a moment her slice of smile falters as Misty and I file inside. She glances between the two of us, calculating who appears the healthiest. I feel like shouting, "If you knew her before you could tell!" I feel angry, but I don't know to whom I should direct my anger. My best friend's twenty-three and has been diagnosed with Hodgkin's Lymphoma. Those are things that happen to characters in Nicholas Sparks books and Lifetime movie heroines, not to your best friend who's more like your sister.

Misty can sense the nurse's embarrassed stare. She raises a hand as if she knows the answer to the question the teacher does not want to ask. "I am the one with cancer."

The nurse nods, her brown eyes melting in tears. "You're so young," she whispers. It is too much. I turn to my right and grip the back of the salon-style chair.

"It's okay," Misty soothes.

Patting the cushioned seat, the nurse says, "Come here, then." Misty plops into it and spins around to face the mirror. The nurse runs her fingers through Misty's thinning red hair.

"It is such an unusual color," she states more to herself than anyone. "Such a shade may be hard to find."

"It's all right," Misty chuckles. "I've always wanted to be a blond."

I laugh with her, in nervousness more than anything, "We'd look like sisters for real, then."

The nurse opens the white double doors to the cabinet and takes down three decapitated mannequins with hair in shades of strawberry blond not resting within God's color spectrum. The nurse peels the monstrosity from the mannequin's foam head and tenderly places it over Misty's hair. The wig's Doris Day cut and Lucille Ball color cause me to smile despite it all.

"Whatdaya think?" Misty asks, puckering her lips and raising a pale eyebrow.

"Beautiful," I retort before we both bathe in the healing Balm of Gilead. Laughter.

FALL 2007

Today, I again sort through my pictures and spread them across the carpet. I smile as I watch these shards of my life falling into place, a mosaic of beauty. There is a new one amid the pile. It is right above the one of Misty and me with our backs to the camera as we sit on the wave-lapped shore of Lake Ontario. The sepia-toned print was taken during our trip to Land Between the Lakes the week before I returned to college for my junior year.

Loading my Jeep with camping supplies and jugs of water, we roll down the windows and prop open the sunroof, letting the wind tease our hair and our laughter. On the dashboard with her slender piano fingers, Misty thumps out the syncopated rhythm to the Last of the Mohicans soundtrack, number nine. We talk of our dream backpacking trip to Ireland, try to answer the question regarding who will be our husbands, imagine one day becoming neighbors who live on vast acres of land with waterfalls, sharing

Sucanat® instead of sugar.

But we do not talk of cancer.

We glide down deserted, pebble-layered roads. A nimble deer leaps in front of my car with the fluidity of a dancer. Yellow birds swoop and dive, making us feel as if we are in a tropical paradise rather than Western Kentucky. Once we arrive at Piney Campground, we unpack our things and lace up our hiking boots. Journeying deeper and deeper into the pulsing heart of the forest, sweat nestles against our spines and our feet begin to burn. A red-tailed hawk spreads its mottled wings and soars. It is enough to make you cry.

The trail curves and opens to reveal a sun-seared, shimmering lake. Crawling down a lip of earth, we toss our backpacks to the side. With our backs to the lake and the shifting sun, we pause a moment, and Misty holds the camera. We angle our baseball caps so that my sweaty, freckled face can be pressed against her own. Misty wraps a strong arm around my back. She is there holding me up, and yet, I am offering her something to lean on. Once again we have traversed the treacherous torrent and made it to shore. With this knowledge, we smile with every fiber of our being — threaded together as best friends, almost sisters — the way it was meant to be.

She then snaps the picture.

This picture was taken at my wedding with my best friend, Misty Brianne Boyd. She's been cancer-free for over eight years.

Jolina Petersheim is the best-selling author of *The Outcast*, which *Library Journal* called "outstanding...fresh and inspirational" in a starred review and named one of the best books of 2013. *CBA Retailers + Resources* called her second book, *The*

Midwife, "an excellent read [that] will be hard to put down." Jolina's nonfiction writing has been featured in *Reader's Digest*, *Writer's Digest*, and *Today's Christian Woman*. She and her husband share the same unique Amish and Mennonite heritage that originated in Lancaster County, Pennsylvania, but they recently relocated from the mountains of Tennessee to a farm in the Driftless Region of Wisconsin, where they live with their two young daughters. Jolina's third novel, *The Alliance*, releases through Tyndale House in June 2016. Jolina blogs regularly at www.jolinapetersheim.com and with other bestselling authors at www.southernbelleviewdaily.com.

*Here it is our
rainy season.*

A Letter to my Sister

Signe Pike

These days I wander no far off lands,
my tales cannot melt hearts and drive off demons.
These days
my tales are of waiting,
like an owl in the desert,
of lucid dreams and tides of connection – you to me – currents
of knowing.

Sometimes these days,
I cry because I have to,
because I feel an end coming to pass
and a beginning, beginning,
and my tears ebb with tides
like salt water rivers
before I choke on them, drowning.

Here it is our rainy season.
We watched the basement sink fill,
spilling over,
creek water cascading
onto the kitty-litter covered floor
soaking our ankle socks,
sending us scrambling for buckets and brooms

as our mother cursed and I threw up my hands because
these days
everything flows
like water.

I sense you like the mourning dove calls
the coming of evening,
in the memories we carry,
the things we've forgotten.
In the haunting coo that invites the night
I listen,
and tucking beak under my battered wing,
I wait for life to begin
again.

*How natural is
all convergence,
the elegant
complexity of
tributaries*

GATHER AT THE RIVER

Michael Bassett

"Soon we'll reach the silver river,
Soon our pilgrimage will cease;
Soon our happy hearts will quiver
With the melody of peace." —Robert Lowry

"We have our loneliness and our regret with which to build an eschatology"
—Peter Porter

Christmas Eve was spent at my grandmother's tiny house
clusters of men spilled across the yard
in the chill and dimly starred dark. The comforting
glow of cigarettes and the heat of political talk
were intimations of adulthood like secrets
from another room at the edge of sleep.

But summers the family reunions
were down by the river at Uncle George's place.
My only brother and I were bred on muted suburban privacy.
One of ten, my father comes from a prolific people.
Labor Days by the river were a riotous rush and swell
of hardly countable and mostly nameless relations.
The rope swing daredevil high above the water
variegated mud and slate and silver,

the ringing of horseshoes and men swearing,
the sticks clanging on trashcan lids as boys played Robin Hood,
the joyous shrieks as children raced
their hand-me-down hula hoops or hooked into catfish.
Later the sun shushed all, baked the word into a torpid dream
with barely the sound of dragonfly wings.
As night approached the musicians began tuning up
to "Let the Circle Be Unbroken."
Three and sometimes four generations, a motley assemblage
of Country, Western, Gospel, Rockabilly, and Blues,
all Pickin' and Grinnin'.

As much as I sensed the magic in it all, I often felt alone.
Clumsy with a rod and reel and unable to draw a bow,
the hunting and fishing culture my dad grew up in
was more alien to me than spaceports in Buck Rogers comics.
Our cousin from Jacksonville, no more at home than I,
at least brought news of fashion trends,
Beastie Boys lyrics, and stories
of knife fights and rollercoaster accidents.

When I read "I Heard the Owl Call My Name" and struggled
with the idea that no community exists
until you suffer together,
I thought of those voices lifted, children in play, adults in song.
What did I know of their sufferings?

The veneration of kin and clan
(as normative as sweet tea where I was raised)
seemed both unmodern and tribal,
at odds with the brotherhood of humanity.

"Some men are born to feel hunted" wrote Loren Eiseley

And I fear it has been so for me.
Yet how unnecessary seems now my self-alienation,
my apartness
that has only recently recognized it is a part of things.
How natural is all convergence,
the elegant complexity of tributaries, root hairs, forearm veins.
How deep the sounding of the river
coursing through us all.

Michael Bassett is a poet, philosopher, booklover, visual artist, and educator. He holds an MFA from Vermont College and a Ph.D. from the University of Southern Mississippi. He is the author of four poetry collections: *Karma Puppets* (2003), *Waiting for Love to Make My Phone Explode* (2007), *A Train Dreams of When it Was a Killer Whale* (2009), and *Hatchery of Tongues* (2014). His poems have appeared in hundreds of journals and dozens of anthologies. He is the winner of the 2005 Fugue poetry contest judged by Tony Hoagland and of the Joan Johnson award. He lives in Bluffton, South Carolina.

Out of the
stillness, the
Tallapoosa
rises.

A BOY IN THE TALLAPOOSA
WITH FLOODWATERS RISING

Fred Bassett

Here in Greenwood, South Carolina, my wife and I escaped the ravages of what some have called the flood of a thousand years. Without doubt, it will be remembered in our state as the Great Flood of 2015.

The only toll it took on me, however, was a lot of anxiety and anguished distress for those hit hard by the floodwaters. It also evoked the memory of my terrifying experience of wading across the Tallapoosa River with the floodwaters rising. I was seventeen-years old that summer. Now after more than sixty years, I think it's time to tell that story. But first, my anxieties about the recent floodwaters in South Carolina.

They started with the ominous weather predictions, while our two sons were in Wilmington, North Carolina, attending a Pop Culture Conference. Jonathan and Michael were both presenting papers Saturday morning with plans to drive back to Greenwood that afternoon. Imagine the difficulty I had keeping my mind clear of collapsed bridges and washed-out highways.

Thankfully, they made the drive back here without incident. Jonathan and his family live near us, but Michael had plans to drive home to Bluffton early Sunday morning.

Six years ago, we bought a little retirement cottage that overlooks a large creek with the remnant of a hardwood forest along its banks. Blue Haven, as we call it, was built on the side of a knoll with the lower side of the foundation within the creek's flood zone.

The big room, which stretches across the backside of the house, has tall windows on three sides, and when I sit in my favorite wing-back chair against the inner wall, I see trees beyond every window. Those trees often host birds of various species, so my binoculars are always handy, but that's a different story.

Early Sunday morning when I looked out on the creek, I was shocked to see that its raging waters were lapping against the foundation of the house. I thought the water might get into the garage on the lower level but would not likely reach our living area, which is a good ten feet above the floodplain.

After that quick assessment, I thought about the townhouses built along the creek only two-hundred yards below us. There was no doubt in my mind that they were already flooded, and I soon learned that those residents had been evacuated by the police before daylight that morning.

Homes were damaged and cars were totaled, but most of the flood damage around here was to our roads and bridges. The damages in other parts of South Carolina, however, were colossal, and no one but a fool could take note of all the personal losses without empathy and a willingness to help. A poet from Ancient Israel summed up that required response with this profound question recorded in the Biblical book of Lamentations:

"Is it nothing to you, all you who pass by?"

The sight of our raging creek helped us talk Michael into waiting until early afternoon to get on the road for Bluffton. Once again, those images of washed-out roads and bridges flooded my consciousness as we anxiously waited. As darkness fell, he finally called to tell us he was home.

The floodwaters of the creek were slowly receding. But the memories they had earlier evoked in me as they tumbled things down the creek were still rattling in my head. I could see myself, a seventeen-year-old boy, caught by surprise in the rising floodwaters of the Tallapoosa River.

The Tallapoosa was the river of my youth. My father took me camping there for the first time when I was six-years old. It had been raining and Dad shut down his sawmill, and we were soon headed for a campsite at the mouth of Corn House Creek. I remember so well sitting between Dad and his two friends as the lumber truck bounded down the rutted dirt roads to the river.

The Tallapoosa was up but not out of its banks. I had never stood on the bank of a river before, and I was awed by its overwhelming grandeur. Around the campfire that night, I watched Dad cook fresh catfish from the river. Afterwards, I listened to the men reminiscing about growing up in the country and then leaving farming behind.

Although I didn't know the word to express it, there was something primal about camping by the river with my father and his friends. That very night before I rolled up in a quilt and went to sleep under the stars, I heard for the first time the alluring call of the wild.

By the time I turned sixteen, I had camped and fished and hunted at a dozen or more places on the Tallapoosa, always the only boy with my father and his friends. Then I started leading my own friends into those same campsites. Sometimes we would camp for a week, living mostly off the fish we caught. And sometime I camped there alone.

The following poem shows, in part, what the Tallapoosa meant to me in my youth. It's also a good stepping stone to the most terrifying experience of my life:

MONKEY MIND

Heraclitus tells us we can't step
in the same river twice.

But what would he say about the same
river stepping in me twice?
It happened just this morning.
But wait! Years ago, I'm waist deep
in the Tallapoosa River on a starless night,
flashlight in one hand, rifle in the other,
wading across to Hester's Island.
On a rock above the swirling shoals,
a bobcat crouches, hidden,
until my roving spotlight shatters
the darkness between us.

Now about this morning. My monkey
mind is jumping all over the place.
High School football practice
in late August, helmets cracking,
boys groaning, retching in the grass.
A seminar on the Dead Sea Scrolls
at Emory University,
Emanuel Ben Dor's voice barking
the Hebrew, resurrecting
those ascetic Essenes, word by word.
Then my mind squats like a frog
in utter stillness. For What?
Certainly not the yogi's nothingness.

Out of the stillness, the Tallapoosa rises.
And there, enthroned above the roiling
river of my youth, that crouching bobcat
quickens yet again the blood of a boy
who once ran wild and unfettered.

What the poem doesn't tell is why I was wading to Hester's Island with rifle in one hand and flashlight in the other. Here's the rest of the story. After spotting the bobcat, I made it to the Island, walked across it, and waded to the opposite bank from my camp. Then I hiked downriver to a large creek and waded up it, searching for fish with the flashlight. When I spotted one resting near the bottom of the creek, I eased the barrel of my .22 rifle into the water and pulled the trigger, killing or shocking the fish senseless. After I bagged two red-eyed bass, as we called them, I retraced my tracks to camp.

Shooting fish that way at night was something I'd learned from an old woodsman who taught me a lot about living off the land. I resorted to this technique only when the catfish weren't biting and I'd given out of food.

Later that summer, I camped above Hester's Island, where the river ran deep and quiet (no singing shoals or rapids). The catfish had quit biting, and I was out of food. Rather than break camp and go home, I decided to hike down the river bank that night to the northern end of Hester's Island, wade across the water, and hunt for fish in the creek downriver.

I had discovered that there was a narrow course that I could wade, just above rapids that crossed the river above the Island, unless the river was up. Above that narrow course, the river was too deep to wade; below it the rapids were too swift.

By leaning into the current and finding a good foothold with each step, I eventually made it to the other bank that night, with rifle in one hand and flashlight in the other. I hunted in the creek for red-eyed bass until I killed two of them. Then I started back to camp, very aware that I had to wade back across the river.

What I didn't know was that somewhere upriver, perhaps as far away as North Georgia, there had been a hard rain and the floodwaters were just reaching Hester's Island. If I noticed that the river was rising when I first stepped back into the water, I don't remember it. What I do remember is that I was soon very aware of the rising water and the difficulty of keeping my footing. By the time that I wished I'd turned back earlier, I was almost halfway across. I was terrified, but I had no choice but to continue.

The river was rising very slowly, but I could measure every inch by the force of the current. I knew that I would be dashed against bolder after bolder if the current swept me into the rapids. At best I would suffer a broken leg or arm, if not both.

Finally, I made it to the bank and climbed out of the Tallapoosa, trembling with fear and gratitude. Do I have to tell you that was the last time I waded the river of my youth?

Sitting there on the river bank, I remembered my father's words after he had scolded me for some risky thing I had done. He said, "Son, you don't know the meaning of fear." Perhaps, that was true at the time. Believe me; I learned the meaning of fear that night in the Tallapoosa. I never told my father, and now it's too late. But I'll tell you to beware of floodwaters. They rise on the just and the unjust.

Fred Bassett is a retired academic who holds four academic degrees, including a Ph.D. in Biblical literature from Emory University. He has four books of poetry, the most recent being *The Old Stoic Faces the Mirror.* His poems have also appeared in more than 90 publications. He has two novels: *South Wind Rising* and *Honey from a Lion.* Fred currently lives with his wife Peg in Greenwood, South Carolina.

the stories
worth telling
no more will
be told

CONNEMARA, IRELAND

For Peter Declan Guy

Signe Pike

The Letterfrack pools are black
black as peat
black-haired like Peter,
this thatched roof cottage, white washed then,
and again,
and now in age,
bathed in bog smoke until our clothing breathed of it,
the fibers filling, the fibers lingering,
aging as we do
in rounds that reach to the Connemara moon,
in sessions that call the slugs to cling
to the sides of the stucco,
climbing to find the warmth
of the fire,
out of the rain
while this old house does what it does
in fading,
in crumbling.
I watched him fix the toilet,
saw him saw a backfield tree
the branches crashing on gravel quarried
from the rough rocks rising from the Bens
weather worn giants of the Celts

weather worn giants of the Picts
weather worn giants laying down their swords
rusting in the rains,
the creatures finding their way through the cracks
slipping into the crevices of
mortar and stone,
weather and bone.

Again and again the fibers burn short,
again and again
the stories worth telling no more will be told,
when nieces and nephews trade spirit for gold
and Peter and Pierce climb the walls with the fierce
snails and slugs that flee from the flood,
flee from the mud, neither Irish
nor English,
neither father nor son,
the threads come undone.

The smoke only drifts from chimney to road,
the stories only fade from wine into mold.
The spine only folds and cracks as it goes
when the songs only echo as long as they're told
the Gull only hovers and the Chough only crows.

> *The heavens open up, and the blessed rain comes down in torrents.*

Rain

An Excerpt from MOONRISE

Cassandra King

The narrator of Moonrise is Helen Honeycutt, the new wife of a well-known and recently widowed journalist, Emmet Justice. Emmet takes Helen to his former wife's estate in the mountains of North Carolina, where a devastating drought becomes a metaphor for Helen's difficult adjustment to her new life. In this scene, Helen, alone in the spooky Victorian estate called Moonrise, is confronted with her worse fears.

It's the brilliant, zagged flashes of lightning that illuminate the stairway enough for me to creep down it, feeling my way with the candlestick in one hand and bannister in the other. I descend the stairs and reach the entrance hall with a sigh of relief, the floor cool on my bare feet, then put the candlestick on the long table under the mirror. I'll pick it up on my way back, after getting the matches. Now that I've made it, and don't have to worry about plunging down the stairs and breaking my fool neck, I might as well get the flashlight, too.

I'm not sure where it is, though, probably in the utility drawer by the stove. Feeling my way carefully, I hug the wall as I go down the back hallway to the kitchen. Even with the bay windows, the kitchen is as dark as the halls of hell, and I fumble my way to the stove. In the drawer I find a full box of matches but no flashlight. Oh, well. Gripping the matchbox like a talisman against the storm, I make my way across the kitchen to the porch on the side of the house, the one where we have our evening meals. From there, I can tell if the storm is going to blow away, or if I'm in for a bumpy ride the rest of the night.

Opening the door leading to the porch, I step out anxiously and look up at the heavy black sky. No rain yet, but the night air hums with tension, with thunder rattling the mountaintops. For the first time all summer, the smell of ozone fills the air. Beyond the driveway, the dark lake roils and ripples ominously, and a strong wind rustles through brittle bushes like the wings of hundreds of vultures.

A flash of lightning hits the ground close by the porch, then is followed by another flash so close that I scream and take off running down the hallway, the porch door slamming behind me. I'm more afraid of being struck by lightning than stumbling and falling over something in the hall. All I want is my bed. Even when I realize that I've dropped the matchbox, I don't stop my frantic run down the dark hallway. No way I'm going back for the matches now—I made my way down the stairs without them; I can sure as hell make my way back up.

Just as I burst into the entrance hall, lightning strikes something out front with such a deafening explosion that I cover my ears and scream again. The entrance hall is suddenly bathed in the flickering light of the storm, and I look up to see a dark figure looming toward me, outlined in the ghostly light from the glass panels on either side of the front door. With a loud cry, I fall backward and lose my footing, grabbing for the wall in a futile attempt to right myself. "Helen!" I hear as I'm grabbed up before I hit the stone floor, grabbed with a grip so tight that I close my eyes and let out another bloodcurdling scream.

"God Almighty," Emmet yells as he pulls me up. "I don't know who's making the most noise, you or the storm."

I've gone limp in his arms, but the sound of his voice surprises me so much that I push away from him wide-eyed. "Emmet! What are you doing here?"

He rubs his face wearily. "I live here, remember?"

I stare at him as I rub my bare arms, smarting from his grip when he grabbed me to stop my fall. "You scared me." I'm still reeling from the lightning and the shock of his sudden appearance.

"No worse than you scared me," he snaps back. Another flash of lightning illuminates his face long enough for me to see his expression. He's furious.

"So you were going to sneak off and leave me without a word," he says in a voice heavy with contempt.

I shake my head, then flinch at another boom of thunder. "No. I planned to leave you a note . . . or something. Then to call you, once I got on my way."

"Once you got far enough that I couldn't do anything about it, I suppose," he says tightly. "Or couldn't follow you to bring you back." Even in the dark, I can see the angry glitter of his eyes as he glares at me. "Know this, Helen. You will never get far enough from me that I won't go after you."

I swallow, and close my eyes tightly. "Emmet . . ." I begin, but he grabs my arm and shakes me.

"Come on," he says.

I don't have time to protest as he pulls me by the arm down the hallway toward the kitchen. "Where are we going?" I'm finally able to ask as I stumble through the darkness in my bare feet, too bewildered to ask more. His only explanation is "Can't see you in there."

Opening the side door, he leads me onto the porch where I just stood to check out the storm. Still no rain, but the wind has picked up, and it blows and howls and tosses the tall trees back and forth against the dark sky. When I realize where he's taking me, I cry out and struggle against him. "No, Emmet! I'm scared of storms, remember? I'd rather go back inside where it's safe."

This time a flash of lightning illuminates the bitter curve of his smile. "If only, sweetheart." His endearment is harsh, not loving. "If I knew a safe place, I'd take you there. But I can't, and you can't do it for me, either, because such a place doesn't exist. Not here, nor anywhere else."

"Emmet?" I say, and he looks down at me curiously. I clear my throat to begin, but don't get the chance.

Both of us jump, startled, at the sound, one we haven't heard all summer—the sudden drumming on the roof of a downpour. The heavens open up, and the blessed rain comes down in torrents. We turn to watch it together, then we work our way toward the edge of the porch, as if neither of us has ever seen such a welcome sight. The sound lifts my spirits and I cry out, "Finally!"

As we stand on the porch and watch the storm rage in front of our eyes, I'm seized by an utterly ridiculous notion. I have no idea where it comes from, but I know it to be true. If I can just feel the rain on my face, everything will be all right. I've been afraid of storms my entire life, a fear that has crippled me, and kept me cowering inside. Without thinking it through, I leave Emmet's side and cross to the back of the porch, where I grab an old windbreaker he left hanging there. After draping it across my shoulders, I return to take Emmet's hand in mine. He looks down at me with a surprised smile that disappears when I yank on his hand and repeat what he said to me earlier: "Come on!"

"Whoa, now," Emmet yelps when I pull him down the rain-slick steps of the porch. He tries to make a grab for the laurel rail, but I hang on tight, and get him all the way to the walkway. Even as he sputters his protests, I pull him by the hand farther away from the house, to the grassy slope that faces the lake. It's too dark to see the lake, but we can hear the sound of the rain pounding it. Emmet's in a dress shirt and his good slacks, and I have on nothing but a thin nylon windbreaker over my nightgown. The rain comes down harder now, beating against us with such a force that I shiver violently, scared half out of my wits. The storm carries Emmet's voice to me when he cries out: "Have you lost your mind, Honeycutt?"

I take a deep breath and release my death grip of his hand. Then, with fingers wet and numb with the cold, I let go of the windbreaker, which I'd clutched to my throat. I don't have to remove it—the wind catches it, snatches it from my grasp, and tosses it aside.

I stand next to Emmet, huddled in the clearing with my silk nightgown flattened against me, soggy grass beneath my feet, and my hair streaming in my face. The rain pounds me so hard I almost topple. But I stand firm, legs apart and arms out for balance. The raindrops sting my skin on impact, like millions of tiny arrows. Then I don't feel them anymore. I keep my head down, and let the water pour over me. Opening my eyes, I raise my face upward, and ask the rain to wash away my fears.

Cassandra King is the New York Times bestselling author of five novels, *Making Waves, The Sunday Wife, The Same Sweet Girls, Queen of Broken Hearts*, and *Moonrise*, as well as numerous short stories, essays, and articles. Her latest release is *The Same Sweet Girls Guide to Life: Advice from a Failed Southern Belle*. A native of L. A. (Lower Alabama), Cassandra resides in Beaufort, South Carolina.

Narcissus,
without water,
may have lived
happily ever
after.

SWEPT AWAY

Batt Humphreys

Water in the best of times, in the worst of times. It is the pool that reflects ourselves, our beauty, our evil. Narcissus, without water, might have lived happily ever after. Bad Nemesis.

Water is joy, and water is pain.

It is the playmaker.

Dazzling from the beach, it offers the dance of diamonds on the surface that comes with the sunrise. And the dare of the midnight swim, and the crazy nakedness of racing to the dunes to taste the salty kiss and ride the passion as waves build and break in union. Then the thief that recedes, carrying remnants of clothes cast aside and lost to the darkness and the tides.

The calm lake on a summer's day is where I learn to water-ski, ever faster, ever daring until the falls become uncontrolled rolls across the surface.

It is white, frozen and crunchy in winter beneath skis and snow-shoe.

Clear, cold speed beneath my skates when venturing onto a frozen lake with miles of open ice and Joni Mitchell lyrics in my head:

I wish I had a river so long
I would teach my feet to fly
I wish I had a river I could skate away on
I made my baby cry

It is the heartbreaker.

Those waves that rise in anger on the leading edge of a hurricane, to thrill surfers before the winds follow and whip water and sand in a horizontal sheet. I have stood in those hurricanes in peril and thrill of covering a story, waiting for the last moment to tuck and run, hoping the shelter would suffice, that this storm in the string would not be my fated one. In the morning—and I was fortunate that there was always a morning after—to witness the tides that took what belongs to them, from those who thought their place and possessions were above and beyond danger.

We have evolved and think we're the precious ones above nature, beyond the water's reach, but we never learn.

The *El Faro* went down with her crew. The high seas as unforgiving as the earliest days of our maritime adventures.

Does anyone know where the love of God goes
When the waves turn the minutes to hours?

It is pure in touch and taste.

It is elemental. It is fundamental.

We evolved from the primordial pool. We are born from the fluid of our mothers.

We've taken its essential purity and made it the cesspool of our waste and disregard, for the flotsam of effluvia we create.

Since 'Silent Spring' we've come to understand it as key to our newly defined ecosystem. We clean up a few rivers, but continue to use the oceans as a dump.

We continue to build, where there is insufficient water to support.

And we watch the polar packs melt, while we migrate and build ever closer to the shore.

Water can be a hard teacher.

We need it to live. We need it to write.

Breathes there an author with prose so dead...who never to himself hath said:

"I've got to get a water/storm scene in here."

Excerpt from Dead Weight

The history of Charleston will have to add two calamitous events.

Both happened in the span of single day. Of Daniel 'Nealy' Duncan you already know. A man hanged as a matter of popular expediency. Yet even as poor Nealy swung from a rope in a stiffening breeze, Charleston was facing the verdict of a higher court. On the night of the execution a hurricane arrived hurtling wind and rain and tide upon the town. A wraith of horrible proportion tore through the streets in equal order. In this town there was no Passover. Nature doled destruction with an even hand.

It will be weeks before the extent of the damage is known. The human toll will not be small, nor will the financial. I can attest to the wreckage of homes and ships. I saw the destruction on the docks of the season's harvest of cotton. There are reports that the city's crop of rice has perished and with it, perhaps forever, the culture of the rice plantation in the South.

In a night, those comforts we take for granted were all swept away. The city that prides itself on its historic roots, was returned to its past. It will be weeks before electricity and telephones are restored to the town. Those who feign gentility will soon find calluses on their hands.

That Charleston will recover is without doubt. The city has suffered far worse at the hands of history. The question is whether Charleston will take pause, to reflect, to ponder the coincidence of events.

There are whispers beginning in the Negro community. They're already calling this the 'Duncan Storm', Divine retribution for the death of an innocent man.

Will the lily-white presbytery of Charleston hear those whispers? Will they connect the acts of Man and the acts of God? In this case, a synergy of destruction, the dominos of Fate that were triggered by a dead weight.

Excerpt from Affair & Honor

Kennedy was floating in the water, in and out of consciousness. He hadn't given up. His body had given out. The current had carried him away from the island and back out into open water. It had carried him beyond the point of caring.

He tried to focus to keep from losing consciousness. That would be the end. Warfield helped for a change. He thought of what he would do if he ever saw him again. Most of the acts were outside his training as a proper son of a prominent family. Hatred is a good motivator, so is love. He thought of Inga, their short and intense love affair, and how much he wanted to see her again. There came a peace as the tide carried him away.

Excerpt from An Untitled Manuscript

Buck Limehouse sat on the dock. It was worn by storms and seasons, like the hand that held the bourbon. The glass was all that stood between decorum and drunk. He finished the contents in one swallow and threw it in the river, then put the bottle between his legs.

The water was high and moving, pulling the dock on the ebb tide, the river returning to the sea. The metaphor did not escape him. The waters were not calming him.

Water is our life...our death, our sin...our soul.

The lips purse as if to kiss, the tongue taps once on the teeth...wa-ter.

It is where I said I love you.

On the river that day. It is where I felt my life begin. It is where I would return to float as ash to the sea. The Alpha. The Omega.

It clinks in the glass that receives my scotch.

I drink you.

Batt Humphreys is the Executive Producer of *Full Measure with Sharyl Attkisson*. Prior to joining the Sinclair Broadcast Group, he served in several executive roles with CBS News. As an Executive Producer he was in charge of *The CBS Early Show*, charged with transforming that broadcast to conform with a revised editorial focus on original and hard news reporting for the network. That drew early and rare positive attention from the *New York Times* and *National Journal*, as well as other publications.

Batt managed a large and diverse staff of correspondents and producers around the world during some of the most critical events of our time, including lead coverage of the early hours of September 11, 2001, several wars, multiple presidential elections and every natural catastrophe known to Man or Nature.

Batt has also redirected a journalist's passion for reporting, to fiction. He has written two novels. His first, *Dead Weight*, was the winner of several national awards. The second entitled *Affair&Honor: Jack Kennedy in World War II* was recently released.

It feels like we are watching music being composed.

ON ALL SIDES WATER

Marjory Wentworth

We walk on planks fallen
over rising water,

weeks of winter rain,
streams on the dirt road winding

through the swamp that fills
then floods then fills again.

Drizzle drifts through
the roof of loblolly

branches. You name
the trees as if they were old friends -

sassafras and sweet gum,
Tupelo and sugarberry.

At the lake raindrops spread
in concentric rings

rippling outward. It feels
like we are watching music

being composed. That's how it is
with us, joy in the rain,

the road back
washing away beneath our feet.

*Water means
love to her,
and so still to
this day she is
drawn to it,
asks for more
water, asks for
more love.*

SUGAR WATER

Nicole Seitz

When I was a little girl, we had a swimming pool in the back yard and a cat who liked to swim. Well, maybe we placed him in the water, and he had to swim? I cannot remember which. All I know is…we had a swimming cat! Which is not the norm. Cats usually don't like baths or rain or such. They much prefer being dry over being wet. Which is why my sweet two-year-old diluted calico cat is so special. Sugar *loves* water.

Sugar waits for me to turn on the bathtub so she can chase the water around. We have to keep her water bowl in there because she plays with it and gets water everywhere. She's even learned how to turn on faucets herself—not a good thing if no one's home. Sugar loves drinking water from the sink and will find an unattended glass of water and just stick her head right in it, thank you very much.

It may be funny to watch, but every time I see this cat drawn to water, I get a lump in my throat. To me, water means Life. Living Water. Jesus is my rescuer, my living water. I see my cat drawn to the water and think of how she, too, was rescued. How she almost wasn't here. How I never would have known her soft fur, her big eyes, her playfulness, her warm spot in the bed.

Three years ago, I came home from a full day of teaching art to children. I got on the computer and checked Facebook. An old friend and animal rescuer had posted a photo of kittens with "Born to Die" above their heads. Apparently, someone had dropped them off at a kill shelter in the Columbia, SC area. At that shelter, a surrendered pet had no chance. It would be "put down" that very afternoon. There were 14 kittens surrendered that day.

At 3:00 PM they were set to be put down. I looked at the clock. It was 2:54. My rescuer friend was in New York, and no one had volunteered to save them yet!

I couldn't stand it. I didn't have time to think, pray, or ask my husband. I contacted the friend and some-

how soon, my sister, niece and I were on our way to Columbia, two hours away. We thought of cute names on the drive there. It was exciting, scary…but it was kittens! Who doesn't love kittens?

We were about to be met with a huge surprise. Fourteen kittens had grown to 23. Twenty-three kittens! We took them all and had boxes of kittens mewing and crying in the back of the car all the way home. Can you imagine such a sound? I would have been in tears, too, if I wasn't in shock. What was I doing? How would I find homes for those kittens?! I wasn't an animal rescuer. I was just a regular person. This was the work for a superhero and at the time, I wasn't feeling it.

My sister offered to take a litter of eight to foster and rehome, and I took the rest. We had a makeshift nursery in the garage for the healthier ones, and the sicker group was on the back porch. After eight tenuous days of prayer, feeding, washing, reaching out to people, vet visits and more prayer, every single kitten found a home.

All but one.

That's when my husband shocked me out of my shoes and suggested we keep it. At this point, I was surprised he would even keep me! We named the kitten Sugar. She is two years old now and full of life and love. She gives us so much joy. When she was four weeks old, out on the back porch, having to be syringe-fed and then learning to eat on her own, she and her siblings got dirty. Very dirty. They used to lie face down in the wet food bowl. I had to wash each of them in the sink daily. And I think that is why my sweet baby is drawn to water. Every day that first week with me she was bathed. She was being loved. Water means love to her, and

so still to this day she is drawn to it, asks for more water, asks for more love.

During the Great Kitten Rescue at our house, we had another cat, Monday, and a little old Chihuahua, Kahlua (Lulu).

We still have Monday, but Lulu passed away last year. A few days before

she died, Sugar went to lie in her bed. She never did that, but now, we couldn't get her out. Lulu wasn't thrilled with her new bedmate.

A few days after Lulu passed away from heart failure, we let Sugar outside. We found her lying by Lulu's grave.

Day after day after day she lay there.

Did she know Lulu was going to pass away before it happened? Did she understand she had died, and her grave was now in the back yard? These are the mysteries of animals and life of death, but somehow I think Sugar knows what it means to be near Death. After all, she was minutes away when I was blessed to rescue her.

It breaks my heart, thinking my Sugar may never have had the chance to live, to give so much to our family. And it's all I can do, when I see her playing in her water, not to run out and rescue more kittens or dogs or what have you. I am thankful there are tireless, passionate people out there like my rescuer friend who do that day in and day out. Because when I look at Sugar, I remember how precious life is, that each life matters, and that all creatures are conduits of love. There is something special about the love of a rescue. It's a river that flows both ways.

*I can trace my
epiphany to a
spring sunset*

My Favorite Thing

Bret Lott

All right, I know it's corny. I know it's predictable, a cliché. But I don't care if I do sound like the usual sap, so truly is this my favorite thing.

I love our sunsets.

Mind you, I grew up with dramatic sunsets. I was born in southern California and was raised both there and in Arizona. I've seen my fair share of extraordinary descents of the sun over the Pacific and the desert Southwest. And when we first moved here to Charleston back in 1986, there was in me a kind of nostalgia for those theatrical, almost garish performances of late-day color against the mountains I'd known in Arizona, and in the magic trick of the sun swallowed whole by that endless expanse of the Pacific.

But then I wised up.

I can trace my epiphany to a spring sunset in 1990 at Alhambra Hall in Mount Pleasant. I'd taken my younger son Jacob to ride his bike on the broad lawn that leads down from the hall to the marsh; he was five, had just gotten the training wheels off, and I took a seat on one of the benches that faces the harbor, watched my son triumphantly execute his first figure eights just as the sun disappeared in the west.

That was when I looked up to the sky above Charleston across the harbor, and the moment when everything changed.

Stretched across the sky above us, and reflected in the harbor before us, was color, every natural color I knew, from the palest violet to the deepest scarlet. And color lay also in the marsh, the sawgrass and saltmarsh hay suddenly awash in umbers and ochres and greens as urgent and sharp as spring itself.

But the strange thing – the captivating thing – was that woven through all this color was a kind of intimacy, a kind of quiet and gentle hand. Here was a harbor, here were church spires, here was the sky.

No rugged geography, no infinite expanse of sea. No theatrics. Only the mystery of colors at once vibrant and hushed at the disappearance of the sun.

I've seen it a thousand times since, this nuanced play of light once the sun has departed: driving the Mark Clark high above the Cooper River, in a jonboat on the Edisto, standing at the end of the public dock at Bull's Island.

But each sunset remains a surprise, and a mystery, and a gift.

Bret Lott has taught at the College of Charleston since 1986, except for a brief interlude when he served as editor and director of *The Southern Review* at LSU from 2004 to 2007. He is the bestselling author of 14 books, has spoken on Flannery O'Connor at the White House, served as Fulbright Senior Scholar and writer-in-residence at Bar-Ilan University in Tel Aviv, and was a member of the National Council on the Arts from 2006 to 2012. He is director of the MFA in program in creative writing at the College.

Indeed, water is the one thing that unites us all.

WHAT ARE WE, IF NOT WATER?
AND IF NOT WATER, WHAT ARE WE?

Julie Cantrell

Water. The very word draws a spiritual reaction. Whether we feel a surge of fear or a burst of awe, the emotional pulse is something to acknowledge. To ponder. Examine.

Maybe there's a reason we experience a primal response when this word is spoken. Perhaps it all goes back to the beginning. Before Eve, before Adam, before anything, there was water.

In fact, water is mentioned in the earliest creation tales, is woven through the texts of every theological narrative, and welcomes readers into the Bible by appearing in the opening sentence of Genesis: "When God began creating the heavens and the earth, the earth was at first a shapeless, chaotic mass, with the Spirit of God brooding over the dark vapors." (GENESIS 1: 1-2)

By the second day, the Bible tells us that God separated those vapors to form the sky above and the oceans below. And by the fifth day, those oceans were filled with life. In fact, water is life. Without it, we die. Without it, we never existed in the first place. Without it, there is nothing but chaos.

And that's the tricky part. Water not only has the power to create. It also has the power to destroy. To return everything back into a "shapeless, chaotic mass" in a matter of moments. And sometimes it does just that.

To the ancients, water certainly represented chaos. It was viewed as a mighty, feral, unconquerable force that could deliver both life and death. Even the gods feared it.

But Christians have a different view. Our Bible deals with water in a strategic way. From the beginning, water was no challenge for our God. Unlike other gods, our one and only Lord, Yahweh, made sense of the chaos. He intentionally, with purpose, brought forth life from the vapors. And since creation, the stories tell us, he has deliberately controlled the seas, the tides, the rivers, the wells.

We see this again and again throughout the Bible, as God uses water to alter man's fate. In fact, God even describes himself as a "fountain of living water" (JEREMIAH 2:13).

When mankind sinks into a sinful, loveless existence, God sends a great flood to destroy his once "very good" creation, instructing Noah to build an ark and begin anew.

Later, God parts the Red Sea, allowing the Israelites to find passage so that they could form a free, missional community and live as God intended. Even their leader, Moses, was saved as an infant when his sister placed him in a basket on the Nile River, a calculated act that enabled him to be found by the Pharaoh's daughter who had gone to the river to bathe. This was the very river her father had in mind when he ordered every Hebrew child be drowned at birth. When the Pharaoh's daughter found the child, she "named him Moses, and said, 'Because I drew him out of the water.'" (EXODUS 2:1-10)

The use of water in this story is no accident. Throughout the entire Bible we learn of waters turning to wine, or people gathering at wells, or even the baptism of Jesus in the River Jordan. It's no surprise that Jesus's first two disciples were found on water or that Jonah's disobedience drew a stormy response from the sea. And one of the most dramatic scenes from the New Testament describes Jesus walking on water. From the very first sentence until the very last book of Revelation, water is used to instill both respect and hope, and when the apocalypse is predicted, it includes a "pure river of water of life, clear as crystal." (REVELATION 22:1)

Water is essential to the stories of faith, not only for Christians but for every religion ever known to man. Indeed, water is the one thing that unites us all. We may argue over trivial matters such as specific rituals of worship, the proper way to dress, or detailed methods to prepare our meals, but strip us of every rule of law, every altar and pew, and it all comes down to one thing: We all need that same clean drink of water. We drink, or we die. It's as simple as that.

But when that life-sustaining substance turns on us, when the tides swell and the waters rise and all that is in their path is carved away with the turbulent tow, how do we process the loss? How can we come to understand, much less love and worship, a God who is mighty enough to stop the seas but instead allows them to wreak havoc on our lives?

One can see the metaphor here. Water, whether literal or symbolic, can serve us or shatter us. And we are not in control of the happenings. But when we do find ourselves in deep, dark scary places, as did the thousands of people who endured the South Carolina floods, we have a choice. We can allow the trauma to harden us or to humble us. And the path we choose will make all the difference, not only for our own lives, but for all who cross our paths and come behind us.

It's easy to aim for humility until we are the ones watching everything we own wash away with the rain. But it's in those times that souls are shaped and lessons learned.

I grew up in Louisiana and now call Mississippi my home. My loved ones know first-hand the powers of a storm. In the wake of Hurricane Katrina, and in the ten years since, I have given water a lot of thought. I even wrote about it in my third novel, *The Feathered Bone*, because the storm shaped me in ways I am still inspecting. In the course of my research, I've learned a few things:

1. Somewhere between 70 and 75 percent of the earth's surface is water.
2. Throughout a lifetime, between 70-80 percent of a human's body weight is water.
3. The earth is a closed system. The same water that existed on the earth billions of years ago is the very same water that still exists today.

Notice anything important here? Maybe it can be boiled down to this: *God created us from the vapors.* That means, we are water. The same water has been on this earth for billions of years. And that means, we are, in a sense, a wave. Or rain. We are a part of the entire creation, which means we have no end. When a rain drop falls to the ground, does it disappear? When a wave crashes against the shore, does it cease to exist? The water returns to the greater collective source, the same vapors that were shaped by the hands of the great Creator. The same waters that formed us all.

Perhaps if we could take a God's eye view, out about 4 billion years or so, we might find something remarkable: *Regardless of when or where or how it happens, we will all return to the sea. We are the sea.*
We are waves. We are rain. We are life.
We are water. We are.
And we are loved.

"But whoever drinks of the water that I will give him shall never thirst; but the water that I will give him will become in him a well of water springing up to eternal life." —JOHN 4:14

Julie Cantrell is the New York Times and USA TODAY bestselling author of *Into the Free*, *When Mountains Move*, and *The Feathered Bone*. She writes for *The Huffington Post* and *Southern Writers Magazine*,

and she blogs regularly at www.southernbellevie w.com. Learn more at www.juliecantrell.com.

I was beyond grateful for my Anchor, even when He "yanked" my heart home.

THE ANCHOR HOLDS

Shellie Rushing Tomlinson

It was the spring of 2011, and we were facing the very real possibility of being flooded by the rising waters of the Mighty Mississippi as it threatened to break through the levee that protects our hometown. I was on book tour at the time and feeling incredibly torn between my desire to honor the last couple of commitments and an increasingly strong pull to drop everything and dash home. I remember a reality-jarring phone call I placed to my darling husband, who was minding our home base on the banks of Lake Providence, LA.

"Honey, do I need to stop and get another generator?" I asked.

(Long Pause) "Baby...if the levee breaks, a generator won't help us."

"Right."

Days later I returned home to join my friends and family in the wait. I stood in a long line and bought boxes, big blue plastic boxes for the papers and the pictures and...and the what? I couldn't imagine where to start. Depending on where we were when the levee broke, if it broke, we could have a day, a couple hours, or seven minutes to get out of town. Really? Seven minutes? Why weren't we already on the road?

In the face of mounting questions that far outnumbered the answers, the words of an old hymn brought solace to my soul, "I don't know what the future holds, but I know who holds the future." I clung to the words of Hebrews 6:19, "We have this hope as an anchor for the soul, firm and secure." It made me think of a boat in choppy water, or more specifically, my Jet Ski that stays moored to our dock during our long hot summers, held by a rope to an anchored buoy. Whenever the water gets choppy the Jet Ski starts drifting away, only to be jerked back time and time again by the anchor. I saw myself in that visual, prayed up and full of faith one minute, only to be sent drifting into the what-ifs whenever the next news report or troubling phone call crashed into my peace. I was beyond grateful for my Anchor, even when He "yanked" my heart home.

As I think back on those days today, I feel for those of you who have lost your homes in the historic flood waters that have recently deluged South Carolina. I'm deeply sorry that you are walking through the tragedy we feared, for when all was said and done our "flood" did not come to pass that anxious Spring. Please know that I fully understand how great a gulf lies between what I feared and what you are facing. For that reason I craft the following words very carefully and respectfully.

You are not in this alone.

There is an anchor for your soul, too. Thankfully, Jesus the God-Man also holds us when what we desperately hope doesn't happen, does. He is a firm and secure rock. Even now, as you set out to rebuild and replace, I'm praying that in the chaos, and the pain, and the confusion, you will moor yourself to this Jesus and let Him be your refuge through it all.

Shellie Rushing Tomlinson is the author of *Lessons Learned on Bull Run Road*, *'Twas the Night before the Very First Christmas*, *Southern Comfort with Shellie Rushing Tomlinson*, and the Penguin Group USA release, *Suck Your Stomach In and Put Some Color On*,

voted Nonfiction Finalist of 2009 by SIBA, the SIBA Independent Booksellers Alliance. *Sue Ellen's Girl Ain't Fat, She Just Weighs Heavy!* was released May, 2011 and has subsequently been nominated for the same Nonfiction Book of the Year by SIBA for 2012. Her latest work, *Heart Wide Open,* was released by Random/Waterbrook March 18th, 2014.

Shellie is owner and publisher of "All Things Southern" and the host of a weekly radio talk show and daily radio segments by the same name. She and her husband, Phil, live in Lake Providence, Louisiana. They have two children and five grandchildren.

*"Don't forget
the treasure,"
she repeated.*

COME THE WATER
Original Fiction

Dorothy McFalls

Rain pelted the tin roof of the Prileau family cottage. It'd rained for so long I could hardly remember a time when I didn't hear that sharp, unrelenting *ping, ping, ping* above my head.

"Come the water to wash away the wicked flesh and all that live around them," G-mom said in the sing-song voice she used when she was talking Biblical. She hummed as she rocked in her ancient maroon lounger. "Only Noah had sense enough to build a boat."

I nodded in agreement. On the TV a lanky man spoke with a quick staccato voice as he stood out in the rain. He didn't need to tell me about the storm. Any idiot could look out the window and see it was raining like all-get-out.

"Girl, ya need to git a'boat," G-mom drawled in that thick Southern accent common to the older folks from these parts.

I turned to gaze in the direction of the lounger. It sat empty. Had been empty for six months now. Still sometimes I heard G-mom's voice as clearly as if she were still sitting there, still quoting her own version of Bible verses.

She hadn't been a kind woman or a forgiving one. But she'd been family. And for that reason alone, I'd loved her fiercely.

I took care of her even though she'd disapproved of every decision I'd ever made. "There you go gallivanting around town dressed like Lot's wife. God'll turn you into a pillar of salt just as sure as I'm standing here. You hear me, Althea Prileau? Do you?"

"You're not standing G-mom," I'd sassed back. "Jesus himself couldn't pry you out of that lounger of yours."

"Don't you dare use His name with me, young lady. You have no right to use His name. Living a sinful life, you young folks do, it'll cause you nothing but eternal pain. E-ter-nal pain."

"I'm going to dinner with a few friends at the only restaurant in this dirt-road community."

"A bar," she'd interjected.

"There ain't anywhere else to go in Jackson Run. And besides, I invited you to come along, G-mom."

"Not to a bar. I'd never step foot into a bar."

We'd had this argument many times those last years of her life. And, as always, I'd cancel my plans and stay home with her. She needed me. And as I'd already said, I loved her.

My friends gradually stopped asking if I wanted to go out with them. Then they'd stopped calling altogether. They hadn't understood why I felt the need to spend all my time with an old crone who'd chase trick-or-treaters off her property with a shotgun.

Losing Heath Roger's friendship—a friendship that had started when we were still young enough to think eating dirt pies was a thing people did—had hit the hardest. Last I'd heard he'd started dating Sissy Baker. And good for him. I didn't want to date him...just be his friend.

"Lying lips are abominations," G-mom said and clicked her tongue.

"I didn't say anything," I answered tartly before remembering I was talking to an empty room.

Since the rains had started G-mom's voice had become even more active. "Althea, Althea! Don't forget the treasure," she suddenly shouted in my ear. I suppose she had to shout to be heard over the pelting rain against the tin roof.

I don't remember her ever talking about a treasure when she'd been alive. The Prileau family never had anything worth anything, other than its family members. And often their worth was questionable. But since her death, the treasure was something she mentioned at least once a day.

"Don't forget the treasure," she repeated.

"What treasure?"

No one answered.

Of course no one answered. G-mom was gone. I was alone. And scared. It had never rained like this before.

In the distance, a whirling wail pierced through the racket the rain was making. A siren? The siren?

Oh...no...the dam.

I leapt from the sofa as if my rear had caught afire.

The rain must have caused the rising water to breach the dam. Why else would anyone set off that god-awful alarm in the middle of a storm?

G-mom was right. I needed a boat.

The shed. I seemed to remember Uncle Johnny storing his old rowboat in the shed. I found a flashlight in a kitchen drawer. After pulling on my yellow rain slicker and purple flowered rain boots, I splashed through the yard. The water in the backyard crick had already overflowed into the yard from days and days of unrelenting rain. Normally, you could step over the water in the crick to get to the other side. Now it resembled a mighty river like I'd imagine the Mississippi would look.

The dam was a few miles upstream from the house. If it failed, I'd need that boat to survive.

Despite the raingear, even my bones were soaked by the time I entered the shed. Cold water dribbled down my back as the flashlight's bright beam bounced off the rough-hewn walls and over the forgotten bits and pieces that had taken residence in the shed. In the back I found Uncle Johnny's wooden rowboat propped up on cinderblocks. Only remnants of its red paint remained. And someone had piled scrap wood inside the boat's shell. I held the flashlight in one hand and tossed the wood to the side with the other. Termites scattered like sailors fleeing a sinking ship.

Please, no. The boat had to float. I needed it to survive.

I tossed the last of the scrap wood aside and placed my hand on the boat's bottom. My palm passed though the wood as if it were tissue paper. No. My shoulders dropped. Rot and termites had destroyed my only hope of escape.

"Don't forget the treasure," G-mom urged.

"Not now," I said.

The road out of the community circled toward the dam before heading for higher ground, so the car wouldn't get me far. I doubted the one-story cottage would provide much protection.

A breached dam would cause a wall of water that could wipe out many of the houses in Jackson Run. Who in their right mind builds a community downwind of a dam?

Oh. Right. Very few in the area had possession of their right mind. Madness must be in our DNA or something. We're our own special kind of crazy in these parts. Some crazier than the others, but always carried with a badge of honor, unless someone starts shooting.

That thought stopped me where I stood.

He came from our community. The shooter. The one who'd killed so many people. That kind of madness that makes someone shoot at innocent people is just plain evil. And he'd been spawned in our community.

I couldn't stop feeling we were all responsible for what had happened. After all, we hadn't stopped him. I'd taught his Sunday school class. Others in the community had called him friend. And yet, no one had stopped him from hating others who weren't like us. No one had stopped him from killing.

We deserved no better than to be washed away in the flood.

Honestly, we deserved much worse.

I stood out in the rain beside the shed, my arms outstretched, watching the waters rise, waiting for Divine retribution to strike. Come the water. Wash away our sins.

I probably would've stayed there until the waters carried me away, but a small mewling coming from down the flooded road caught my attention first.

What was that? An animal?

I lowered my arms and followed the sound. The water had risen so much so when I walked it sloshed over the rim of my rain boots, soaking my socks.

At the end of the muddy driveway, I found a car with its front end buried deep down in a ditch.

"Help us!" a man with skin as dark as the flooding waters called from the front seat. Rising water poured into his open window. A woman waved frantically from the passenger seat. Something small was clutched in her arms.

A kitten?

No, not a kitten, I soon discovered, as I helped pull them from the wrecked car. A baby. A tiny baby with a wrinkly face.

"Do you have a boat?" the man asked, his voice tinged with desperation.

"'Fraid not. And no car will get us to high land."

"What will we do?" the woman cried, holding her baby closer to her chest.

What will we do? I asked myself. I had to do something.

"Don't forget the treasure," G-mom admonished.

"This is more important," I said.

"What?" the man asked.

"We need to get help." I could call my friends.

No. They were busy. They had to protect their own property, not worry about me. But then I looked down at the baby wailing in the worried mother's arms. Rain washed over his blue-tinged cheeks. He wouldn't survive long in the rising waters.

I dialed the first number that came up on my cell phone. Heath answered on the third ring. I told him where I was, who was with me, and how the boat had a hole.

"My God," he breathed. "The dam—"

"I know. We're about to start swimming here."

"Get on the cottage's roof if you can," he said.

"I'll try. But Heath, there's a young baby. He needs—" It was too silent on the other end. "Heath? Heath?" He must have hung up.

"What did he say," the man demanded.

"He suggested we get on the roof."

"Is someone coming for us?" The woman's voice warbled.

"I don't know." I truly didn't know if anyone could get to us. But the baby, the poor innocent baby didn't deserve to die like this, no one did.

With the man's help, we swam into the shed, which was nearly under water by now, to retrieve a ladder. By the time we'd returned the young mother was holding her baby above her head to keep him above the splashing water. The man insisted on holding the ladder steady while the young mother scrambled up the ladder with the baby tucked against her breast. The turbulent waters from the dam had grown so high around the cottage it threatened to wash us all downstream, but the man was strong. I managed to get myself onto the roof before the ladder was lost in the dark hungry waters. The man wasn't so lucky. I reached out to try and catch him.

"I could use your help, G-mom," I whispered...a moment later my questing fingers wrapped around the man's wrist. With a strength I didn't know I had in me, I gave a sudden yank and pulled him from the mouth of the waters and onto the roof.

We were safe, but for how long? The baby's cries were weakening.

"Have faith in the treasure," G-mom whispered.

Faith? I didn't even know what the treasure was. I hunched on the peak of the roof brooding. Treasures were useless to lives in peril.

"A boat!" the man shouted. I heard a soft whir of an engine before seeing a large blue boat as it labored upstream toward us. All my friends were aboard: Heath, Angel, and even Sissy.

Thank you, G-mom. We were saved. I was the last to make the jump into the boat. As soon as I landed, Heath wrapped a wool blanket around my shivering body and pulled me into the circle of his warm arms.

"I thought you were with Sissy," came out of my mouth before I could even stop myself.

"We went on a couple of dates, but we both realized my heart was waiting for someone else. And what a time to be asking about that. I'm awfully glad you're safe." He kissed the top of my head as Sissy steered the boat downstream.

A week later and with Heath and Sissy and Angel at my side, I returned to G-mom's cottage to survey the damage. The cottage was gone. Holding my hand to my throat and tears in my eyes, I wandered through the thick mud that covered everything on G-mom's property.

I didn't feel her presence. Nor did I hear her voice. I hadn't heard it since the day of the flood.

It was gone. All gone. *G-mom was gone.*

"Look," Sissy said and pointed to something down by the crick. I shivered as soon as I saw it. G-mom's maroon lounger had been stranded in a pile of mud at the edge of the shoreline.

I slid down the muddy bank to get a closer look. A book sat open on the seat of the lounger. It was one of G-mom's handmade books of inspirational quotes. Though damp and thoroughly ruined, I could still make out what was written on its open page. "A faithful friend is a sturdy shelter; he who finds one finds a treasure ~ Book of Sirach 6:5–17."

We might have suffered and lost. But thanks to G-mom, I had

found her missing treasure. Despite our flaws and imperfections, we were blessed in this dirt-road community of Jackson Run because we had each other.

Dorothy McFalls makes her home on the coast of South Carolina with her husband, two dogs, fluffy cat, and adorable baby. In 2001, she took a leap of faith and pursued her dream of writing romantic fiction full-time. As Dorothy St. James she also writes cozy mysteries. Reviewers have called her work: "amazing," "perfect," "filled with emotion," and "lined with danger." Learn more at www.dorothymcfalls.com.

"It's in God's hands," I said.

THE LONGEST NIGHT

Dianne Miley

Hail pelted the windows in the middle of July. Lightning pierced the pitch black night. The wind whistled and howled. A clap of thunder jolted me straight up in bed.

I heard my mother crying. I was seven years old. The year was 1969.

We didn't have early warning systems or cell phones. Our family was so poor, we didn't even have a house phone.

That night, we didn't have electricity either.

We had no way of knowing what was happening in the northeast Ohio world outside our windows – no way of contacting anyone – no way to reach my father.

We didn't dare walk to the neighbors' house. It was the middle of the night.

Hail turned to pouring rain – rain that came down in buckets and wouldn't stop – rain that flooded our yard, our driveway, and our neighbors. Branches, hunks of bark from our sycamore tree, and slabs of shingles from our roof sailed through the air like missiles in the roaring wind.

Lightning splintered the black sky, lighting up the yard outside our darkened windows. I stood against the back of the couch, staring out the window. I cried for my daddy and watched for any sign of his car, any car, any sign of life across the wind-whipped and water-logged landscape.

Thunder cracked with booming ferocity.

I nearly leapt from my skin.

"Get away from the windows!" My mother picked me up and set me and my little sister on her lap in a chair across the room. We watched the dark windows.

Each time lightning lit the flooded lawn, we stood for a better view.

My mother told us to go back to bed and not to worry. But I could tell she was scared. Her voice cracked and her eyes were red and watery. I heard her crying before, even though she pretended everything was fine.

I didn't want to go back to bed. I wanted to wait up for my daddy too.

My mother didn't argue too much. I think we kept her company and made her feel a little less alone and scared.

My father worked second shift from three o'clock P.M. to eleven o'clock P.M. in a town eight miles away. Only eight miles, but that night, it could have been the other side of the world. He should have been home hours ago.

So we sat in that chair, my mother, my sister and I, in the middle of the night, and prayed.

Over and over, I prayed the same thing.

"God, please bring my daddy home."

"God, please keep my daddy safe."

"God, please bring my daddy home."

I don't remember what anyone else prayed, I didn't know what else to pray. I begged and I cried and I prayed some more.

Eventually, I must have passed out from sheer exhaustion.

I woke up in my bed and it was daylight. I jumped up and ran to the living room.

My mother sat huddled in the same chair.

"Is Daddy home?" My heart filled with hope. He had to be home by now.

"No." My mother sounded so defeated, so small and scared.

"Where is he?" How could Daddy still not be home?

"I don't know."

But she was my mother. She was supposed to know these things. How could Mommy not know where he was?

I climbed into her lap. She was utterly depleted. She couldn't hold her tears back now.

We prayed again, desperate and deflated.

"Please, God, bring my daddy home."

My sister and brother woke up, young children who wanted fed. My mother went through the motions, feeding us bowls of cereal with cold milk and closing the refrigerator fast because the power was still off.

The scene outside was bleak. Huge limbs lay across our driveway. The entire yard was covered with water and debris – branches and bark, shingles and siding floating through the yard.

The morning hours dragged.

Daddy did not come home. Depression set in.

Where was he?

Was he dead?

NO. I denied it.

Please, God, bring my daddy home.

My prayers grew increasingly desperate – begging, pleading, in denial that something horribly dreadful had happened to my father.

Nine o'clock. Ten o'clock. Eleven o'clock.

Please, God, bring my daddy home.

My mother still wore her nightgown. She was unresponsive, nearly catatonic with shock and fear.

Please, God, bring my daddy home.

My mother prayed. She read her Bible. We kids sat on the floor, not really playing, not really doing anything. We just sat there in shock. We didn't know what else to do.

So we prayed too.

And then we heard it.

Sometime between eleven o'clock and noon, we heard the crunch of gravel, the sound of an engine, and water sloshing.

We flew to the window, stumbling over one another.

God brought my daddy home!

We ran into the flooded yard in our bare feet and pajamas.

Daddy was haggard, for sure, exhausted and rumpled.

"Where were you?" my mother screeched. And then she hugged his neck so hard that he couldn't answer.

My father laughed. "I couldn't get through," he explained. "The roads were flooded. Uprooted trees and downed power lines blocked other roads. Every way I tried to come home, I couldn't get through."

He'd driven out of his way for hours in the wretched storm, on every road he could think of to get home. Finally, it was raining so hard he couldn't see, and he was so exhausted that he shut off the car in front of an uprooted tree that blocked the road. He slept in the car.

In the morning, he walked to a nearby house and found someone to help him move the tree so he could get through. Only then he came to another roadblock, and another. Eventually, road crews began clearing the trees and the electric company began removing downed power lines.

My father picked his way home, stopping to move trees and limbs, and detouring around flooded areas miles beyond the eight mile journey.

Arm in arm, we walked inside.

We later learned there had been a freak tornado that night. Many in our small town of Perry, Ohio lost their homes – some flooded, some obliterated. Some friends at church had the roof torn off their house in the middle of the night.

We were wet and we needed repairs. But God answered our

prayers.

We picked up branches and bark for days. We didn't have power for three weeks. But my daddy came home, so that was okay.

We never gave up praying on that longest night.

And God brought my daddy home.

Forty-six years later, I had another longest night. Rain poured down in Mount Pleasant, South Carolina. Rain for days, rain for hours, and the ground was saturated. Twenty-four inches of rain were recorded at Boone Hall Plantation across the street. Long Point Road was flooded. We heard a police PA system telling people to turn around throughout the day.

Across our yard, many puddles became one unending stream from our front yard to the side yard and all the way to the back. The flooded area grew deeper and wider as the hours ticked by. By late Saturday night, our front sidewalk was covered, the landscaping against the side of the house was saturated in standing water to within two inches of the siding, and the driveway was under three inches of water.

Water seeped under the garage door, and flowed all the way to the back wall where the garage meets the house.

At eleven-thirty that night, my husband and I mopped and squeegeed the water out. We placed bags of soil (all we had) against the seal of the garage door, and turned on a big fan.

We moved our furniture away from the exterior walls and rolled up the rug. Then we sat on the couch together and prayed.

That's not to say we hadn't been silently praying all evening long.

We'd done all we could do.

It was one o'clock A.M. High tide would reach its peak at one-thirty, and we were exhausted.

"It's in God's hands," I said. "If water gets in the house, we'll just have to clean it up."

Our home was in God's hands, and he would take care of us. I went to bed with a sense of peace.

Sunday morning, our floors were dry. The water against the house had receded a bit. The garage had dried out.

But it was still raining.

My husband bought a pump and began pumping water from our side yard to the storm drain on the street. He pumped water all day Sunday and kept up with the rain.

Another longest night was over. Once again, God heard our prayers and protected us.

Yet if our home had flooded, would that mean he hadn't protected us?

If we live, He is with us. God is good. "And we know that God causes everything to work together for the good of those who love God and are called according to his purpose for them." —ROMANS 8:28.

What if we'd been caught in swift water and drowned?

"For to me, to live is Christ and to die is gain." —PHILIPPIANS 1: 21.

God's love never changes, no matter my circumstance. From the tornado in Ohio when I was a girl to the flooding in South Carolina many years later, it's my faith in Christ that's kept me afloat.

"And because we are his children, God has sent the Spirit of his Son into our hearts, prompting us to call out, 'Abba, Father.'" —GALATIANS 4:6

Dianne Haynes Miley lives near Charleston, South Carolina with her husband and mother-in-law. She and her husband grew up in northeastern Ohio where they raised their now-grown son and daughter. She enjoys spending time with her family, walk-

ing on the beach, swimming, reading, flower gardening, entertaining, hosting tea parties, cooking, decorating, and traveling. In addition to writing, Dianne works at a Christian pregnancy center where she encourages young women in unplanned pregnancies. She founded a non-profit, Sanctuary Of Unborn Life (SOUL) with hopes of building a maternity home in the Charleston area. A portion of all her book proceeds benefit SOUL. To learn more, visit www.diannemiley.com where you can find her books, sign up for her quarterly newsletter, or connect with her on Facebook, Twitter, Linked In or GoodReads.

we paddled our
kayak through
a set of French
doors and into
the great room

THE BEST NATURAL DISASTER EVER

Sarah Loudin Thomas

We'd had floods and hurricanes before Floyd blew through Conway, South Carolina, on September 16, 1999. As a matter of fact, I owned my very own pair of chest waders. They were camouflage and while I would have preferred another color, they kept me dry when I had to park my car on the paved road and wade the quarter of a mile in to the house overlooking the Waccamaw River.

Someone once asked me if I ever worried about alligators as I slogged through the water. Well, I didn't until then.

Floyd didn't amount to much in the way of hurricane winds, but it surely did dump an excess of water into Lake Waccamaw upstream from us in North Carolina. The problem with rain in a place where the land is flat and near the ocean, is that runoff has nowhere to go.

Although our house sat on a bit of a rise near the river and was a good three feet off the ground, the water just kept coming. We moved what we could to a neighbor's second story bedroom. We wrapped the legs of the poster bed in trash bags and piled belongings on counters or on top of furniture we never liked that much anyway. We loaded clothes into more garbage bags and stowed them in the kayak with our three dogs.

Then we abandoned ship and drove to my in-law's in upstate South Carolina.

When we returned a few days later, the water was still rising. My car, parked in the front yard, had water up to the steering wheel. We grabbed a few more things and moved in with my dad in Conway where the town's founders had the good sense to find a bit of high ground.

When the water crested, the only part of my car still showing was the tip of the antennae. Water in the house stopped just shy of the light switches. On a perfectly sunny, early autumn afternoon, we paddled our kayak through a set of French doors and into the great room. Light reflected off the water and shimmered across the vaulted ceiling. There was a stillness. An odd sort of peace.

That was in September. Less than four months later, in January of 2000, we loaded what we'd salvaged into two cars and a moving van and drove to Western North Carolina where we had a new house and new jobs waiting for us.

The house was the first one we looked at; the jobs the only two we applied for.

Sixteen years later I'm serving in a children's ministry, writing Christian fiction, and active in a local church. We're closer to my husband's family, and he's found ministries of his own where he can make a difference.

We still look around at the beauty of the mountains and the changing seasons and marvel at our good fortune. Neither one of us misses the ocean or the flat land or the long, hot summers. We feel like we belong in this place where the land rises and falls away again in permanent waves.

And all it took to move us, was a natural disaster.

"For I know the plans I have for you," declares the Lord, "plans to prosper you and not to harm, plans to give you a hope and a future. Then you will call upon and come and pray to me, and I will listen to you. You will seek me and find me when you seek me with all your heart." —JEREMIAH 29:11-13

Sarah Loudin Thomas grew up on a 100-acre farm in French Creek, WV, the seventh generation to live there. Her Christian fiction is set in West Virginia and celebrates the people, the land, and the heritage of Appalachia. Her third novel, *A Tapestry of Secrets*, will release in August 2016. To learn more, visit www.SarahLoudinThomas.com.

*God had wooed
me from my
plan to His
purpose.*

INVITATION OF LOVE

Denise Hildreth Jones

I'm a planner. And right now the plan was in the wee hours of the still dark morning to finish packing this cooler at my feet, pack the car, then make my way back to the hills of Tennessee from the panhandle beaches of Seaside, Florida. But there was a stirring I couldn't shake. An invitation that tugged. *Let's go see the sunrise over the ocean.* That wasn't the plan I reminded the tug as I grabbed more items and stuffed them into the cooler. It tugged again. *Let's go see the sunrise over the ocean.* I surprised myself as I struggled through the tension of my plan verses this proposition. Surprisingly, the proposition won. I grabbed my earphones, my phone, and a large cup of hot tea. I drove down to a private pavilion. Didn't look like anyone else was crazy enough to be awake at that hour, so I assumed freedom and took my uninvited self to the empty Adirondack chairs.

The sound of the waves as they met the shore was so tender. They lapped. They didn't roar. The sound was similar to the invitation that had fallen on my heart. Gentle. Constant. Inviting. The week had been so full. The ministry I lead had just finished one of our Weekend Experiences, and I had poured out for four days. Every piece of my heart desired to know that I had been pleasing to the heart of my Father. In my responsibility of having to "see" people and minister to their needs by being connected to Him, I was left needing a moment to feel "seen" myself.

I have spoken for years of how God loves us in our details. Have had countless personal stories of my own that have told of this detailed love and have heard countless others. But in this quiet soaking, my heart was so full. Yet still in need. I read my devotional out loud for me and the creation whose hearts remember and long for His return too. Then I stood to my feet and walked over and down the walkway to get a better view of the sun as it began to unfold itself to greet those of us wild enough to be waiting for its arrival.

The song came unexpected. It passed from my lips before the words had yet to truly pass through my mind. They came from an instinctive place. A holy place. Holy, Holy, Holy, Lord God Almighty, Early in the morning my song shall rise to thee. This place was holy. The majesty of the water before me, the invitation inside me, the beauty of all I had seen God do in the lives of so many over the last few days, all of it demanded one word alone, Holy. It had been holy. It was holy.

As the song came to an end and as I leaned by body across the railing to take in the massive body before me I spoke these words, "Father, the one thing that would just put the finishing touch on this weekend and just speak so loudly that you are pleased would be to see some dolphins out there." I didn't know where that had come from either. But it flowed straight from my lips and from the deepest place of my heart.

Watching the water, a sea of glass, I continued to hum as the waves lapped in a melodic rhythm. Then my eyes caught a glimpse of something about a hundred yards away. "Is that a fin?" I wondered. I peered harder. I saw it again. Now, I'll be honest my first thought was not dolphin. My first thought was shark. So, I am assuming that it was probably a very good thing that I was the only one out there, as me screaming, "Shark!" might have messed up a really profound moment. But then I saw another. And then so slowly, so gently, with a soft rise and fall, one dolphin, then two, then a third began to make their way up and out of the water. And with each rise and fall they moved closer to me. Before long they were rising higher and higher. For over twenty minutes I watched them until they finally swam out to sea.

Had someone been near me they would have watched a grown woman weep over this display of love. God had wooed me from my plan to His purpose. He had shooed me from my doing into simply being. And in the middle of it He had delighted me with the knowledge that He sees me. He who spoke that massive body of water into existence loved me enough to stop the world to speak His detailed love to my needy soul. In those twenty minutes He filled up every empty place with an indescribable love.

I had stared over those waters for twenty years, but in that moment, what He allowed me to see held more love than had I seen dolphins every time I had ever looked. In our empty moments, in our needy seasons, in our soul thirst, the Creator of our Soul, the Father who spared not even His own son to capture our hearts, woos us. And I have learned that when God invites and we respond, He reveals Himself every time. This time it was in the ocean by a beautiful dolphin. It has been many other things since. But this I know, my sweet friend, no schedule is too important, no demand too demanding and no need too great that responding to His invitation of love won't be worth it each and every time.

Denise Hildreth Jones is President and Founder of Reclaiming Hearts Ministries based in Franklin, Tennessee. She is a wife, bonus mom to five teenagers and a playmate to a really cute Shih-Tzu. She loves Sunday dinners with her family, soul conversation with her friends, reading good books and cold Coca-Colas. And every now and then she writes a few books. www.reclaiminghearts.com

After the water
I feared
It might never
return

ONCE

Eva Marie Everson

*The town I met my husband in (and where we lived for 15 years), flooded in
1994. Graves popped open. Houses were washed away. The house I lived in when
I first moved there was flooded, which made me sad. It was a great cabin on the
Kinchafoonee Creek. I hope they were able to preserve it a little.*

I feared the water
Once
I feared the weight of it
The way it swirled, forming tiny tornados.
I feared the way it rushed in
Water over water
The swishing and gurgling of it
I feared the way it rose

I feared the water
Once
I feared the thievery of it
The way it came in, stealing things
My home and
Those items I can never replace
I feared the way death smelled

I feared the water
Once
I feared the way it shook open

The graves of those long buried
Coffins bobbing
Along the river it formed
I feared the way it floated

And then…

After the water I feared
It might never return
Never bring a shower on a hot day
To cool things down and
I feared I'd never
Run beneath it
Giggling like a schoolgirl

I feared I'd never, ever
Not even once more
Find myself caught in it
Clothes stuck to my body
Hair slicked to my head
Droplets clinging to my lashes

I feared I'd never, ever
Not even once more
Run headlong into a puddle of it
Feet jumping firmly into its center
Ripples upon ripples to the edges
I feared I'd never again leave my mark

I feared I'd never, ever
Watch it form rivulets
Streaming down my windowpane
On a chilly spring day, inviting me

To lie nearby and read a book or
Take a nap

But then the rain came
A summer shower
A lovely shower
Dripping off the eaves and the leaves
Turning greens greener and blues bluer

And me?
I opened my arms to it,
Laughing, laughing...
No longer
afraid

Eva Marie Everson is a multiple award-winning author, speaker, and teacher. She is the president of Word Weavers International, the director of Florida Christian Writers Conference, and serves as education consultant to SON Studios. She is a wife, mother, and grandmother who, for all practical purposes, is owned by her dog.

God is here in the water, in the trees.

Our house is a river where books have gathered in great piles along the banks

How natural is all convergence, the elegant complexity of tributaries

It feels like we are watching music being composed.

the stories worth telling no more will be told

"It's in God's hands," I said.

Don't assume that what was ordinary yesterday will be ordinary again.

She holds me up, yet I give her something to lean on.

Out of the stillness, the Tallapoosa rises.

Water means love to her, and so still to this day she is drawn to it, asks for more water, asks for more love.

we paddled our kayak through a set of French doors and into the great room

The rain comes hot with fury.

Here it is our rainy season.

After the water I feared It might never return

I can trace my epiphany to a spring sunset

I was beyond grateful for my Anchor, even when He "yanked" my heart home.

Indeed, water is the one thing that unites us all.

I have found it to be true that disasters bring out the best in people.

God had wooed me from my plan to His purpose.

Narcissus, without water, may have lived happily ever after.

"Don't forget the treasure," she repeated.

The heavens open up, and the blessed rain comes down in torrents.

Printed in the USA
CPSIA information can be obtained
at www.ICGtesting.com
LVHW091914100424
777042LV00003B/58